More Praise for Little Domesday Clock

"Is it possible for a book to be both terrifying and enchanting? *Little Domesday Clock* is—I felt as if I had entered an ensorcelled place, that space from which all those forces now contending in the most urgent life and death ways for the very soul of the planet are being amplified and projected. If the earth has a score, it sounds a lot like this. Sam Witt's brilliant, imaginative book puts to shame much of the current vogue for a poetry of social mission—it invents our moment for us. I'm grateful."
— DAVID RIVARD

"*Little Domesday Clock* is a brilliant, sweeping book which, like a time machine, transports a reader back and forth across boundaries of nation and history and, in doing so, exposes and indicts the human agency behind disaster."
— LYNN EMANUEL

Series Editor: Andrea Selch
Title Editor: David Kellogg
Design: Lesley Landis Designs

Cover Painting: ©2015 Clay Witt
"Sister Moon, Brother Crow"
Cover Photograph: Jay Paul

Author Photograph: Clay Witt

The mission of Carolina Wren Press is to seek out, nurture and promote literary work by new and underrepresented writers, including women and writers of color.

Carolina Wren Press is a 501(c)3 nonprofit organization supported in part by grants and generous individual donors. This publication was made possible by ongoing support made possible through gifts to the Durham Arts Council's United Arts Fund.

Library of Congress Cataloging-in-Publication Data on file.

PCN: 20179528857

ISBN: 978-0-93211-279-8

Little Domesday Clock

Sam Witt

Poetry Series #19
CAROLINA WREN PRESS
Durham, North Carolina

"For as the sentence of that strict and terrible last account cannot be evaded by any skilful subterfuge, so when this book is appealed to its sentence cannot be put quashed or set aside with impunity. That is why we have called the book 'the Book of Judgment' because its decisions, like those of the Last Judgment, are unalterable."
— RICHARD FITZNIGEL, 1179

"It is only our conception of time that makes us call the Last Judgment by this name. It is, in fact, a kind of martial law."
— FRANZ KAFKA, *The Blue Octavo Notebooks*

ACKNOWLEDGMENTS

I wish to thank the members of the Fulbright Selection Committee and the Institute of International Education for awarding me a Fulbright Fellowship to St. Petersburg, Russia in 2002, during which time the germ of this book was conceived.

For my family, and for Stuart Wright, whose support and influence I have neglected to acknowledge for too long. In memory of George Garrett, a great teacher and a great writer who is sorely missed. Thanks to D.A. Powell as always, gentle reader and friend. In memory of David Bromige, for his work, and for pointing out that poems can rise. Impossible without Mary Ann Lugo, Bruce March, David Reid, Jayne M. Walker, Tala Hadid, Tom Yiull, and Kevin Prufer. I also have to remember Reginald Shepherd here, a great poet, a great supporter and friend. Thanks to the entire English Department at Framingham State University, especially to Professor Patricia Horvath. Lastly, I have to thank David Kellogg and *Carolina Wren Press* for making this book more than pixels and words. Thanks to Jamie Keene, who is an invaluable friend and artist.

Grateful acknowledgments to the editors of the following journals, in which these poems have appeared: *The Briar Cliff Review*: "Occupation: Dreamland"; *The Laurel Review*, "Ten Tweets from the Future" and "Moonlight in the Body of the Lyre"; Pleiades: "Thermal Signatures (Helios/3:58)" and "Icarus, in Moonlight"; *Crazyhorse*: "The Aphasia Ward"; *Denver Quarterly*: "Thermal Signatures (8:46)" [original version] "Thermal Signatures (19:19)" and "Seven Tweets from the Rapture" which was first published in a small collaboratively published journal put together and distributed by Carol Ciavonne, entitled *Dritto;* *Colorado Review*: "New Moon"; *Meridian*: "Frankenstein; or, The Presence Chamber" *Fence*: "Thermal Signatures (1:28)"; *Los Angeles Review*: "Little Domesday Clock: Stroke the Tenth: Love in the Anthropocene"; *The Iowa Anthology of New American Poetries*, ed. by

Reginald Shepherd: "Thermal Signatures (8:46)" [revised version] and "Thermal Signatures (16:31)"; *Boston Review*: "Toxic Assets," "Little Domesday Clock: Stroke the Eighth: Poet of Underwater Cities," "Nine Tweets from the Tribes of the Unconceived," and "Nine Tweets from the Seraphs." In addition, "Little Domesday Clock: Stroke the Ninth: The Timepiece & the White Whale" was long-listed for the inaugural University of Canberra Vice Chancellor's Poetry Prize in 2014 and was published in the *University of Canberra Vice Chancellor's Poetry Prize Longlist Anthology*. "Nine Tweets from the Seraphs" was long-listed for the 2017 University of Canberra Vice Chancellor's Poetry Prize and will be published in the 2017 Anthology, entitled *Iris*.

"The Aphasia Ward" was written in a collaborative effort with the photographer Melanie Flood, reproduced along with her photographs in *Abe's Penny*, and mailed to subscribers as postcards. "Little Domesday Clock: Stroke the Tenth: Love in the Anthropocene" was the winner of the Red Hen Press Poetry Award for 2013; the judge was Hilda Raz. "Occupation: Dreamland" was the winner of the *The Briar Cliff Review* Poetry Prize for 2007. "New Moon" and "Icarus, In Moonlight" were reprinted and posted as voicefiles on *From The Fishhouses* (www.fromthefishhouses.com)

Table of Contents

Frankenstein; Or, The Presence Chamber

Among the distant
inequalities of the ice
by some law
in my temperature
I was so guided
with a child's blindness
picking up shells
like a child
And thus for a time
was occupied
by exploded systems[1]
till I beheld a stream of fire
issue from an old
and beautiful oak
by such slight ligaments
that even then
hanging in the stars
I was now alone
in his kindling eye
Angel of Destruction
Useless elixir of life
Invisible world
with its instruments
of bringing to light
Derange their mechanisms
that the stars
often disappeared
in the light
of the structure
animated
to the receptacle
of bodies
I was alive

---

[1]   #govt.whitepaper, #weatherischanging, #stomach: Follow me @Iamthebomb ·
7:42 PM, 19 May 2013

Which brooded over me
White and shining
pyramids
Giver of oblivion
Take their rise
in the icy wall
of the glacier
overhung me
the silence
of this glorious
presence chamber
I saw felt heard
and smelt
at the same time
between the operation
of my dark
opaque bodies
feeling pain
and a radiant form
rising among the trees
The little winged animals
who often intercepted light
broke from me "Fire"
"milk" "bread" "wood"
was Father
although I longed
more deeply
to discover myself[2]
when the heavens
poured forth water
was starlight
of my creation
or creator
I wept
this being
You must create
among the undulations

---

2   We are singing our own extinction—Dr. Vandana Singh · 1:06 AM, 30 Nov 2013

of the sea of ice
the corpse
the monstrous Image
the disastrous future
And I seek
the everlasting ices
of the North[3]

Here's an actual view of a massive iceberg shearing away from Antarctica: http://bit.ly/2INfMRS • 6:00 AM, 25 Feb 2017

FOUR
THE HELIOS OFFERINGS:
BLACK-EYED CATTLE OF THE SUN

~

Μηδεν Αγαν
NOTHING TOO MUCH[4]

---

4   I am the Alpha Soul, the Uber-mensch, the Unterman, the fail-safe
Omegamale: Western black rhino declared extinct http://www.cnn.
com/2011/11/10/world/africa/rhino-extinct-species-report/index.html?s-
r=sharebar_twitter · 2:54 AM, 31 Oct 2013

Little Domesday Clock
Stroke the First: Starter's Pistol

In orange jumpsuits & replication machinery,
in toxic orange clouds released　by the blasting caps:　in dead zones,
　　　　　　　　　& jellyfish fields submerged, blooming us
　　　　　　　　　@a_coupla_leagues_under_the_sea,
under the deep-sea tethers of offshore oil rigs　(how the jellyfish love us)
　　　　　　　　　The people are a missing chromosome.
　　　　　　　　　Where do chromosomes go when they die?
In isotopes & Mnemioptic binary code,　encyclicals, gargantuan icicles,
　　　　　in sickle cells:　0, 1, in gene editing:　in lipids & sugars,
　　　　　　　　　0, 1, I, we, the ongoing verb,
　　　　　　　　　in 160 mph winds, in storm surges
that carry diseases, we　　0:　are pollution pulses
1:　are　fully saturated phosphates, freshwater fluxes　0:　fleshwater.
　　　　　　　　　X marks the spot on the brainscan.
& through slats　in the　platform girders, before the rig exploded,
0:　you could see the bright blue　waters of the Gulf below...
1:　in fadoms, pink swarms of harvest flies, in the fiberglass cotton candy
　　　　　　　　　between the walls, in neonicotinoids,
infested lavender clouds, in thousands of dead honeybees
　　　　　　　　　literally vomited out of the hives:
　　　　　　　　　in vast chemical screams:　We:
1:　a crown of gulls over the landfill, a tumbler remark, 1, 0: just a smile:
0: a hollow cry: 1: shot through with　oceanic starlight
　　　　　　　　　& cool liquid distance:
　　　tick, tick in 1, in 1, in 0...
　　　　　　　　　The people　are ghosting again[5]
in spiral torsion, spools, minute watch pins, *tick,*　in a big fat gold zero,
　　　　　　　　a hinged pocketwatch: tiny quivering coils, spring steel, 0, 1:
0:　in an underwater 37.5 mHz pulse, that same frequency emitted by the
cockpit flight data voice recorder: *ping*　　*ping...*　We the Black Box

---

5　　BTW: There's plenty of room for us in the sky · half a minute ago via web from
　　Weymouth, MA

We the PPL   are the *bomb*.   A dirty bomb that is: the f-bomb
                             going off in the Promised Land: I, We, 0:
        for the sake of our children,   0   0   *tick, tick*   We
                        feed on one another: We
                        the Damned: We the Happy
(happy as a tick full of blood,   a   Lone Star Tick   that is,
                        small white zero on the dorsal shield) a
timebomb,
just *tick, tick, ticking*…were the   spillover moment,
                        the runaway: the tipping point: de boom.
All the clocks say: *Go to sleep my little babe*
Sweep   my little second   hand   toward the 0.   & just like that,
that never
                        that sleep: that hero.
                        For infection[6] (O my 1, O   my   zero)
                        in the sentence   breeds

---

6   Hey! When we talk Little Ice Age, you'll need to remember this: There is a
     Moment in each Day that Satan cannot find · 1:43 PM, 20 Oct 2016

The Aphasia Ward

The sea is approaching. Ghostcrabs   approach
on whispering feet, white froth,   static,   acidic gray waves, white noise…
A young woman   steps forth on a whisper of sea grass,
                              holding a blank camera.
Now.   *Click*   & again,   now   *click.*
I am not going to *say* these syllables: & again, the voice of one saying
   Cry   ticks you out of this place, back into it,
a minute explosion,   *click*   a sudden freezing
                              into this precise coordinate:
   When you first stumbled across that small heap of decay
—black feather, hollow bone,   these small dead—minutes ago,
                              camera in hand,
   it must have looked like a sweater for a small child,
or a black bra the sea had washed up in.   So it glows far up above,
the Shining beachfront   Hospital   on a cloudforest Hill,
                              & a bald eight year old girl
                              watched a speck   fall out   of the sky
into the ocean, then another & another,   then closed her eyes
         with each beep[7] :   into that immaculate white room
                              surrounded by eucalyptus trees beyond the glass…
I was sleeping, as they say, under the wing.   The voice of one saying: *Cry.*
         What shall I cry?   That all flesh is black grass?   *Click*
                              That all flesh goes the way of flight, even yours?
Once it's been evaporated? Now that the camera has fired off?
                              The clock been impregnated?
Unlike these dead waterfowl, fresh from their migration flyway,
We come preforgotten,   a photograph of a dirty beach:
bottles, syringes, plastic agricultural wrap.
                              We   come   out of   a nowhere,   we are
         a kill-cry in the shape of these tern,
                              a series of—*click*—beeps.
They perfume my loss.   They appear   out of the shining white.
They make me want to shed my   triploid   gene with a click, a flash, a blink,
         a beep, beep,   a wish,   falling behind her closed eyes.

---

7   & we breath in our sleep, & we wade into the ocean only to wake up, & when we open
         our eyes · Sun Sep 19 2010 23:40:50 (CDT) via web from Framingham, MA

& the girl counted each   one from her starched bedsheets as they dropped
                out of the sky.
You could almost hear the sea's   ceaseless mathematics from the beach,
                from that cloud chamber in the Aphasia Ward
from this white   space assembled out of the small sounds
                the girl was making in her sleep.
The sea turns over   its dead.   The sea
washes its white & dark digital hands   of us at noon,
                in foaming little 1's & 0's.
The sea was ready to deliver its dead in   binary stars (in seconds) at noon.
The sea conjugates its dead
                in flight & falling,   in decay &—*click*—
The sea operates   at the cost of a   young   woman's exact substance,
    at the cost of a girl-patient's   *click*   extinguished language,
            the cost of...   disappearing locked away
                inside her shiny pink dome,
eroded (with the coasts) because already, you've cast her liquid shadow
down below you at noon, in glossy ink: already you've spilled Her language
in bird-shapes, unrecognizable consonants, strange sounds,
white uncurlings, in fallings,
                a photographer's black hood
                thrown down over that small avian corpse,
then another.   The little girl saw it all   from her hospital window
        before she ghosted you.   & just like manna
                the birds continue to fall, one by zero by one.
Because they eat you in   those small   black eyes
        where they carry entire, momentary skies   entangled with the cells
                Of other migratory eyes.
We take the light with us therefore when   we fall.   Therefore,
                the starched hospital beds are filled,
                emptied[8], filled. Thus,
they move us onto your curled, glassy paper, freeze-look, star-eater, click.

---

8   It's like this secret, private little nightmare & you can't do anything about it · 2:03 PM,
    10 Nov 2013 from Manhattan, NY

How the wind   in the eucalyptus leaves kept moving my wrist into
these black V's, kept moving her small lips

until she closed her eyes.   Made a   wish.   Slept.
We   went out there   for   good   together:
                    Quietly   alone
behind the pink eggshell of her   powerful forehead[9]   Thus
the sea negates   the sky because   living   hell
                    (& dying   too)

        it's something   like swallowing jewels isn't it?

---

9   Depriving a poem of the white space that surrounds it is like depriving a tree
         of darkness · 6:42 PM, 7 Feb 2017

New Moon

It just slipped off my wrist & glinted a last time
on its way down, sterling silver disc, cold new moon unseen,
disappeared into the waters when I was nine,
at the beach.   & for weeks after,
I could hear my father's wristwatch ticking at night,
big as the ocean, from the heart of the whale,
as my breathing slowed... That woman
for instance has gray-blue arctic eyes[10]
when the sky begins to burn off its heavy water at dusk
& the pond glows a melted sapphire freeze.
That woman opens her eyes somewhere out there,
in the desert.   Her gravity turns me even now,
nights I slip from her wrist out of bed, thousands of miles away,
then rain down her dry cheeks. By the pond, therefore,
in the dark,   I open like a moonflower. Her face is gone now
but it speaks to me in extinct light.
I'm still rooted like a waterlily into that disappearance when You,
Black Moon, slide down the tree limbs unseeable,
a majestic liquid Being poured from tree to tree
through this deciduous portal, tethered to invisible black fire.
Try to think with your skin she said.
Close your eyes. Slide down the snapped tree limbs
but it's too late. It takes a long time
to burn a mammal's heart, even at full fadom tonight,
as long as it takes the missing moonlight
to search the black corridor of a deer's pupil, then move on
once the bodiless jewel has spilled liquid
out of my eye in a single
whisper You leave behind in this flesh, ghostly female,
psychic whisper hollow as a god & just as massive,
Speak darkly of shedding because,
because—when I remove my socks, my jeans,
I'm tearing off a bandage slowly.

---

10   The people have a camera implanted in each eye, oh yeah & we steal these
        tangible pictures of a world we can't quite reach · Mon Sep 20 2010 17:57:44
        (CDT) via web from Framingham, MA

You cannot enter the sky by wading into this pond,
though the clouds hang here suspended above the lemon trees
like cottonballs in formaldehyde.
In black liquid fire it tells me,
You're trapped, by the light of ten thousand sins, in a body.
You can't simply go away just because this damaged self wades off.
The entrance to the kingdom of heaven is everywhere
like the new moon but you can't
just because you contain the sky, enter it, not down here,
swallow it, say, not when salvation is saving up light you can't,
is swallowing an ocean in a gulp,
not when the missing light bathes you in its cold
Red-tailed hawk's cry, swift, unseen, *keer!* the kind
you can't hear when *you're* the prey,
when the forest consists entirely of poisoned rain
& the horizons touch nothing but themselves & melt
& even her blue iris simply vanishes like a coastal shelf, or a city,
with its voices, into the sea—when sound
shall escape these words, the ultimate moment comes.
I will call my pupils Stargazer Lilies until then
because they open in the night, they look forward
into shattered starlight below me, far into the past.
They feed on this new lost light & after.
They navigate by the starchart gone out
in her drowned eye, a tiny replica of the sea,
a life-sized map of deep space expanding.
Speak to me in distant breathing over the telephone.
Speak to me through this extinct hiving,
Stargazer, terraqueous globe, desert honey, wild splintered bloom,
forest eye's view, bedroom-sphere, speak me up until now:
all the wiped out honeybees have surrendered
into an oceanic droning within us[11]
We will inherit the Kingdom of Oblivion.
The insects shall inherit the earth.

---

11   You give yourself away to a deeper noise inside them, the score of a silent
      movie: #PurestOfHolyFires: This man throws up his arms/a woman
      screams/cut to 3rd face · Mon Sep 20 2010 17:58:42 (CDT) via web from
      Framingham, MA

Icarus In Moonlight

It was the weight of the child in her belly[12]
caused those wings to fail Icarus, in moonlight
but then, *my* heart writhes tonight
in skyfuls of falling bodies luminously cold.

That's why each splash of hidden light,
in a trick of the eye, comes like a young woman with wings
falling into the sea tonight, out of the new moon.
Why it projects me forward into a single,

deranged—until this missing beam
has searched my eye, then my veins for a sea to fall into
& moved on, once the sky
is shedding the sky in unimaginable bodies,

turning in a low nocturne of exhausted moonlight
disappeared on these pages for a fading second.
Some nights, when I write too long,
hunched over the lunar papers, a sharp jagged

aching shoots up & down my right arm
from the place in my shoulder blade
where cruel boys pulled out an appendage.
Then these exhumed pages must serve as wings,

coming apart in the gun metal light,
now that I've come out here, as I often do,
into the woods, by the lake, by Blood Creek
to track the hidden new moon by its gurgling.

---

12   Which, as far as I'm concerned, is the same bolt of cloth: The dead cry out
      against us: the dead feed on our open mouths like gallons of heavy cream ·
      11:10 PM, 16 May 2013

But then, the sky has shed
its luminous daughter through *me*
at the rate of a missing orb & tonight
it does not rise.

The only hint of a maze under *that* moon
was the way sea & sky continued to reflect one another
in her eyes as she fell, the way it had become entangled
in that umbilical cord but still

the foetus jumped within her
in a sudden weightlessness that consists of how
right now, the actual moon drifts,
unseen, lost in the black waters of my pupil.

If you could have seen her,
turning in that videotaped footage at the Ministry of Fates,
could have looked through the closed-circuit security camera
as Atropos, the Unturning,

looked through the unscarred lunar face
all those millennia ago & with a solitary glance,
cut her thread, you'd have seen her black hair
unspooling out behind her in a horse's drowned mane

as she collapsed against the apex of her flight,
feathers, melted wax, & falls once more, released out of the sky.
Maybe you'd have turned away too, as that newborn celestial did,
to hide its suddenly pocked face in darkness—

as it has every thirty days since then,
out of pity. New light will bubble up within you instead[13]
now that you're reading this, like a teenaged girl
struggling for air as it rises into the sky,

---

13   Through which the people advance in little corpses & starched hospital beds
        & plastique figurines moved around the chessboard desert by a little girl ·
        Wed Sep 22 2010 10:49:32 (CDT) via web

climbs the snapped branches out into the open
& as you kneel here with me before the lake, bursting with air,
your wrist comes back up coated in silt,
disturbs the rotted leaves just under the surface but then

we can't *see* this pale disc after all,
spring of its wept light, disfigured source. Not tonight.
You can only hear the splash of a Smallmouth Bass
—she must have been a big one too—

breaking free of the surface to jump clear, flash silver,
then disappeared back into the center
of that widening circle,
the hole that closed around her,

& the waters of the lake heal themselves.
Not on this Thirtieth Night.
It shall remain concealed but then

You carry the gene for falling[14]

---

14   ~~Even though we're tempted by this godspace to rise~~ Before the drones could
realize their mistake, the aptly named Hellfire missiles rained down ·
10:41 PM, Sep 19th via web from Framingham, MA

Dark_O_the_Moon

Like the moon we grow out of a nothing.
Like the new moone this black veils a cold buried radiance
to which I shall return in hir arme.
I am genetically unquiet in the shedding light.
I won't notice when the last star
goes out in my eye, evaporates the blood like invisible ink
in the final vanishing act, whose vaporizing gaze
the invisible orb merely feeds tonight.
I am a child of the unborn thereof,
because always I wear my own dying of which my birth consists
& it feeds me to the borrowed wounding
that runs like an underground stream.
I was born by the river   I am the echo of
& like the river iver   *I've been running ever since*
You can't hear those cold waters in real time
of course. But thrust your hand
under the iced-up surface of the creek,
& it'll clutch your wrist alright, carry you off to the apparent event horizon,
where unseen digestive juices dissolve slowly the city into tiny bubbles
surfacing in the sea-bed view.
For slowly the sapphire hour had begun to bleed out
a wild virgin spring bubbling my heart away slow.
Already it has burst. & like a blister she bled out alright,
legs spread right there on the pool table,
no teeth, a local, goes by the name Dark O' the Moon,
when the poolroom goes dark & they're waiting, & one by one
everybody gets a turn[15].
For our souls shine not through our chests.

---

15   Quite simply, the people would be forgettable ~~in drams of depleted uranium, white hot phosphorus, strontium 90~~ were it not for their pain · Tue Sep 21 2010 3:39:53 (CDT) via web from Framingham, MA

Never the moon drifts in & out of place unseen,
anchored to that portion of sky
where I'm invisible: Back there, beyond the beyond,
the moon projects us along this fine edge & in a few weeks,
the sky will wear us in a thumbnail the way I wear pain,
which is to say, on the thin edge of the wedge,
I am a mere trick of the light
until these robotics cease our respiration.
Black light, go on scanning my scraped out veins.
Rifle through me with such weight
that it has turned this lunation inside out.
Carry me away by the impending invisibility.
& the sky's missing bells are gonna ring out
when the entrance to the kingdom appears
in a cloud of vaporized butterfly wings but for now,
a single white leaf turning its hidden fires should do—
turn this window in my chest until it corresponds to oblivion
until my tongue's been preserved in fireweed honey.
Speaking waters, come near my lips, cast me through them
in little shaved-off crescents that fall away, like us, us.
& when I sing, useless & gorgeous as a Mockingbird,
the body of its orb nowhere to be seen,
Obliterate my mouth into a cold exfoliating language
that sets the trees on fire with wind.
It's fiftie fadom deip.
There's a destination inside the acid grammar
of this redacted light but you don't want to know what it is.
Look, something's shining in the creator's hand[16]
Look, already it's gone out.

---

16   The people have blunt features like a composite police sketch, or a bubble
      rising in cheap champagne · Tue Sep 21 2010 21:59:57 (CDT) via web from
      Framingham, MA

Open this one place being mostly us : by forgive, I mean, I am Explosif

River of Smallest Combustion, Sun Being, rise
The Helios offerings[17]
     & forget, of course. O gods ye gods of mine, give me poison, poison!
I mean, Go now & open : as Lethe passes through me, I member
     Alleyway—He—carbonhemmorhaged—Ol factory of Japanese Cherry
                                                     Trees—Ios—Is
     When the man driving past cries *Forgive* through his bullhorn
& the emissions rise westward in little waves of the Choir Invisibule
     When the street wears me on its little finger: shall go

El : Not empty but peopleless gapes its lovefeast: shall go
                  Before meltdown before capillary before *before :*
    Syllable of a new tissue : Hel—
         & black letters were falling down my blankness:
              One line rising from another
Drift up the page, stupor,
                with heaviness with child with embryosia of steam,
      Seapt into our monokrone, where shall I go my son?
        The sun being has fallen: invisible emissions
       The son of Helios has fallen in a sewage updraft.
    For the light was more than I could bear O steeds of fire[18]
    Beasts fed full of ambrosia, black sky beyond the neon glow.
         4 times 3:58 from an immortal dawn.
             2 minutes from 4
          By the alleyway that agapes
           I mean, Sip of this exhaustif
        Orange peels fall lightly on my head.
         In the Alley of Smallest Appearances
    Stationwagons. Exhaust. Avenue of Steam. Market Street.
         By forgive, I mean…sewage updraft.

Thermal Signatures

                                            3:58 /Heliopolis

---

17   When I undress the polyaromatic hydrocarbons in heaven · 1:03 PM,
        21 Mon Apr 2014
18   I am explosive when I undress the skies · 1:04 PM, 21 Mon Apr 2014

Little Domesday Clock
Stroke the Second: The Secret

The West Antarctic Ice Sheet   O my Disappeared Fates

                                    hangs above us

by a single shining hair.

           Take the Eastern Anatum Peregrine falcon

(now extinct)   suspended in flight

salmon pink, a white coverlet over its cere.

                      Whisper the secret into its ear

through those imagined

              auricular feathers: *where are you going?*

Speak into the planetary sink:

                         "Love, love, love…"

You are bowls of fire my people,

                     when the sun sinks low.

You are a comet tail, fading on the azimuth

at sunrise[19] but where?

                   Drift along an ocean thermal

with the White-Shouldered hawk

                (endangered) & you'll come to it,

the secret of our eventual birth,

                 suspended in thin corrosive air

like a guillotine blade.

           You didn't half keep it from yourselves, did'ya?

                   The way this all ends?

All of us afloat in fields & fields of babies,

                       smack (in-gasp),

a smack of jellyfish & bawling.

              You were all poison, the Great Killing,

the Sixth Mass Extinction, a pall,

                    O my disappeared…

You were a single incandescent radioactive thumbprint.

---

19   Now my capillaries are woven into the Sirens' silks O my people · via web ·
12:27 AM, 15 Apr 2015

You were all the extinction verbs spoken at once,
species-hush, a wish,
                        spirit hordes blowing off *sotto voce*, mugshots
merged en masse, a touched bell.
                        How the emissions sang your manacles
in the combined faces of criminals,
                        in the choir:
in Amway commercials, advertising jingles,   DNA traces,
                tiny links, Ace of Spades up your sleeve. & later,
blind in the blind, O my people,
                        my Great Dying,
it came for us too.
                        You were such a small breathing nihil
at the heart of the mall.
                        This was where it ended:
in such massive arcades: You & you & you,
                        & the dead
were an invasive species. You:
                        a tiny deadly bubble
carried back up to the shuddering heart
                caressing & untying that bloody knot
& you, & you &...   POOF[20]

---

20   Tell me the word known to all men: WOR-ald without end · 12:26 AM,
        15 Apr 2015

Nine Tweets From the Tribes
Of the Unconceived

That weight in your crown, that visitation—it's not the 471 lbs. of pressure exhibited during parturition—but the weight of those of us who shall never be born · 9:27 PM, 14 Sep 2013 · 2 minutes ago via web · Embed this Tweet

You who came hurtling headfirst into the world, who speak in extinct words, you, who whistle along with the extinct nightingales · 9:33 PM, 14 Sep 2013 via web · Embed this Tweet

All the bells that never rang multiplied by all the little deaths unconceived=a teaspoon of collapsed star embedded in your brain=this ghost thinking=this nuclear waste · 9:40 PM, 14 Sep 2013 via web · Embed this Tweet

We the Unpeopled, tribes of unwatching: smell of petrichor as we hit the cement with the rain & you realize the parking lot under your feet was virgin forest · 9:54 PM, 14 Sep 2013 · 2 minutes ago via web · Embed this Tweet

In the time it takes your phone to change "sentence" to "semtex[21]" a species of glowing fish goes out where your finger stops the spinning globe ·10:06 PM, 14 Sep 2013 via web · Embed this Tweet

& that bioluminescence whispering—entirely produced by bacteria—that pale vanished breathing we shed over your lives, 'tis an aposeopesis not precisely unlike a melted glacier ·10:10 PM, 14 Sep 2013 via web · Embed this Tweet

Me: I don't want to live in a world without elephants. The voice on the phone: Is that an ultimatum? · 1:51 AM, 11 Jan 2014 · Embed this tweet

---

21 These computers are beehives in which we store an ancient vanishing honey: silence, language, coordinates · Mon Sep 20 2010 17:57:49 (CDT) via web

Am I to understand the entire suit lapses & melts away? Pal, away. Bye bye Greenland, bye bye Green Bee-eater, no more sunshine, it's followed you away · 3:03 PM, 5 May 2014 · Embed this Tweet

Write it out in disappeared words: I wish for the life of me there was not a clock in the kingdom to measure out these drams of oblivion. For the oceans—[22] ·10:13 PM, 14 Sep 2013 via web · Embed this Tweet

---

[22]   —the oceans are a life-sized map of themselves as they die: All in a wave now, lift your wigs to show the pink dome of the world as it crowns · 9:28 PM, 14 Sep 2013 · 2 minutes ago via web

Thermal Signatures: Circe

Herein yes I circle below   I   wander   on my back
Below: the tatooed artery pulses   below your long translucent neck
Below: @zero on the bed   I wand   at ero s   as
                                as above/so below   speaks the zeroeros
                                the hero: speaks yesterdays of affliction
Speaks the ripped   ultraviolet   to a fingertip falling   I below.   So
you trace my blue circle you circe   as below/as low in the wavelength
                                so a light-tap from the aftertime
speaks my muscular eyelid be-blind   unbind its low frequency below.
                                We have coupled to an unterchild
            in undertime: you enter me below   in its dark band of color
                                I beg an arterial quiver low[23]
                    I smile through your sleep   & you wand me
you want through my   neck   roomb to motherlay these deepest petals
into a warm place called NEK TAR   untrace me its warm Circe below
You wound   You unwand me into this place you unwound
                    Where to speak is to quiver something new
                                Our dystopia : as above/so above
Our dystocia circles me livinglessly a baby was
                                You carry in your mouth below
Digested into the birthpangs of where I was : us : as : above : was :
                                amnion : amnow : &—
Didn't I wander then?   Not even at a touch?
                                Hasn't the ingrown sky crept into my preborn brain?
With corrosive whispers? *sugarliftshallbeee?*
                    Didn't I stand at warm   zero   then   *shall   speak?*
                    Speak soft tissue & sleeper cells?
                Cover my blank face of noise with a hiving yes esse
Enter me@one finger per second   yes
                                liquidated through warm aftercircles
Yes   its as below branched   into the arteries in my otherNek
                                The dancing is contagious
                                A dead fly lies bellied on the sill
& she felt it too
Divested of her eggs days before   her work   done   NEK :

---

23   Do genes "remember" pain? Scientists suspect they might · 12:09 PM, 19 Dec 2016

(that which overcomes)   TAR :   (death)
                         in its 16 fingered centiclusters
       It stumble heavily   It buzz the flat glass face of the sun *Oh*
                         through our sleep yes it sloozes me
       sunsubtombed   on my green back below at 4:32 p.m.
          of the nuclear   ombansflower   that moves[24]

---

24   Look through your own eyes: Ready to do the shuffle & coil? · 8:13 PM,
      27 Dec 2013 via web

These Pages Have Been Redacted

The Secretary Of War (1)
Presidential Daily Brief

The Secretary of War is an animal under moonlight O wondrous [~~...~~
~~Father redacted...~~] she prey. Every animal shall be a pure underexposure
of God's face.

That's why, ~~when the Secretary of War~~
~~weeps in the moonlight~~, & her cheeks run black with tears of light, sweet,
etc., she knows the President by name, well enough to say 'We are all
animals' in code, '~~swift in the pursuit.~~'

The President is a life-sized map of the veins in the human body. All the
arteries are missing from this map. But the Secretary has all appropriate
access codes *Lest there be an opportunity for draining*

This first bit of prayercode has escaped her thin photocopied lips & can
only be read in a shroud of moonlight:

"In the beginning God created oil" reads, in darker encrypture: "And
God said, Let the waters under the heaven be gathered unto one place"
and LOL! half a world away, light, sweet crude did bubble forth from the
sacred underground bunkers. "And the evening and the morning were
the third day," right to left, decoded into mirrortime, the times & half
a times read:

~~"Ladies and Gentlemen of the Desert, either you accept our offer of a~~
~~carpet of gold, or we bury you under a carpet of bombs."~~

That was the code: Black Gold, Texas blub-blub, liquid 1's & 0's,
slow tears a-bubbling up through a gash in the side of the desert floor...

"Evertime I see those refinery hammers going, it's like they're pumping
my heart." But why speak of it? The President's blood in the piss of
the body politique, like ruby fluids, like pomegranate seeds in oil? Of
neon blood, pinkish white skin, Old Glory, denim blue skies, the river
Jordache, cover ~~& baptise the bodies as they come home, still immersed~~

~~in bullet-time,~~ that point through which reality flows, &, &, Let them exude the perfume of war as they fall, each according to the gravity of his own faith, as our heroes fall: "~~Show me where they are & I will kill them,~~" said the man with a laptop on horseback &, &…

~~[I suppose I am also the secretary of war.]~~

Only when I walk under this black light can the access codes be read, the ones I keep buried under my skin: come home from that bullet-still-point from which we, animals, be ciphered, boys, children, into rivers of smoke, the shape of smoke the eagle screams, the eagle guzzles 20 million barrels a day, ~~Children Operation Infinite~~ be screamed into our bodies in freedom smoke: ~~Only then do the codes lightly hiss a gold-composted, agonal gasp: G=D…]~~

We interrupt this prayer to bring you…Green plastic hoods! Stacks of vacuum packed cash on pallets drifting down to the desert floor on parachutes from the skies.

[…onely in the moonlight can these lines of code tattooed on my forearm be read:] ~~Clandestine, foreign government, and media reports indicate~~————this binary, this broken naked man, head covered in a green sandbag, in green night vision.

Look through the blacked-out eyes of the disappeared in which I am together, alone, mama, papa, Mr., Vice, light, sweet, crude fire from the parted heavens will fall————in green night vision

at \$31.05 a barrel, to \$35.95, to \$69.47 etc. will fall, Father, Son, to \$118.75, mama, rising through broken airwaves, my love, my wife, shall fall as black rain, with all its tiny, neon rainbows blacked-out until only the cost of flesh remains——~~Objective: Akron Objective: Toledo Objective: Charleston~~——~~Objective: Boone~~ a body, a severed thumb, a thump in the sand, belonging to a child,

~~O my nation, abomination: the Adam Bomb: the Atom Tomb…~~

THREE
OCCUPATION: DREAMLAND[25]
(Book XI, The Odyssey)

~

Εγγύα πάρα δ' ἄτη
GO BAIL AND DESTRUCTION IS AT HAND

~

"But this is History. Distance yourselves. Our perspective on the past alters. Looking back, immediately in front of us is dead ground. We don't see it, and because we don't see it, this means that there is no period so remote as the recent past."
— ALAN BENNETT, *The History Boys*

---

25   What is the meaning of a pure color experience, this spectacle, this crack in the sky & a hand reaching down to me? · 6:39 PM, 16 Nov 2013

Occupation: Dreamland[26]
for Garrett Scott, November 19, 1968 – March 2, 2006

Those boys, the ones you filmed in Fallujah,
they were drowning too. That's why
when they patrol the streets of that desert city
in night vision, in your film, I can't watch it anymore
not without feeling this pressure
behind my eyes & inside my ears for softly then,
you opened your mouth *inside* the god,
at the bottom of the deep end, breathed a huge lungful
of water; but in here, the sunlight
slides in at an angle through the leaded windows
to the rustling of fir needles & here I am
at a writers' colony, 6 weeks after I met Lt. Basik at your wake,
on crutches because they had to amputate his foot.
It's unthinkable: to be the very first to have filmed
an I.E.D. exploding, not 60 feet away from your humvee,
only to return to San Diego a year later
& have a heart attack in a swimming pool.
Lie back, turn onto one side, carry a palm across my chest
in a free-style crawl. The pressure just grows.
When I press my palms to my ears & cry out,
trying to feel each auricle with fluid submerged,
all I can hear is each second curiously undoing the next
but instead of water flooding into your lungs, it's sunlight,
God's syrup, come streaming through this window,
released from that moment your heart exploded
without a sound (though *my* eardrums are ringing still),
from that place where you wait at the deep end without a body,
to fill this room with shining.
There's a crucifix on the wall, missing its christ.
I wait here too in an empty bed, a human pudding

---

26   Isn't it amazing? The marketplace—despair, consumer impulses, climate,
        grief, the occupation of a country, pain, this isolated episode of transient
        global amnesia—was us · 5:52 PM, 24 Jun 2013

the ooze in your golden locks
has been laved into, into a nectar,
scratched by the scamper of a squirrel's feet on the copper roof,
the sound of those locks being picked. Open up.
The god will still be screaming at his feet, deaf;
this clothed, naked ape
still occupying the bed instead of ash,
chips of bone, preserved in honey in a funeral urn.
& your body sinks so decisively
to the bottom, even though
they've already divided up your ash between them:
one syllable cancels out the next
to the tune of the sidling light, the pearling
of a turtle dove, the weeping horses.
It is blood that is streaming & blood that is spilled[27]
You can see right through it, like water, or air,
having passed back through my lungs,
& so it has been twice made,
at the exact same weight we shared, 49 kilos,
once for you, once for me,
& the balance of that weight now
is zero. I can feel it, a little tremolo when I talk.
& if *somebody* has been erased,
replaced by these glittering needles,
then it isn't hard to imagine
that everything, just this once, has been uncreated,
especially this copper light, that kneeling inside of it
would be like kneeling underwater,
& to cry out when you did as it withdrew[28],
leaving behind this alienated substance
in the place of your body, in which I lie,
it's like touching the copper mask of my own face,
through which I can see drops of sap burning in the late light,
a sleek honeyeater,
balanced with its tail against the trunk.

---

27   & if they had slashed my throat all the way through with Occam's razor, if I
      were in the form of a blue embolic sphere, in short, if it were positively dil-
      linger! One big tickle! · 6:15 PM, 24 Jun 2013
28   Keats: Some have died before they were conceived · 11:47 AM, 20 Jun 2016

There's a tiny waterfall in the distance, silent & white.
I have come to occupy this body for a while,
where the smeared face of it goes on this piece of paper:
"I have many faces, but only one is branded to my skin,"
even as the light completes its favorite trick
of draining away. The occupation begins now,
in a darkened room: I am wakened again
into my fear of touch.

Thermal Signatures: The Owl Of Minerva Spreads Its Wings Only With The Falling of Dawn

There is nothing to remember but flight,
The owl spread its steel & titanium alloy wings.

Come with me on my flight to oblivion,
The owl's eye slowly blinked, head cocked, feathers of iron[29]

I watched its clockwork eyelid lift & fall. I watched its eye
Tracking me through the grey tinted glass on the 70th floor.

Spoke flight & onely through its mechanics, brutally,
The owl's gray eye spread in joules of silence:

Only with the falling of dawn
Does the owl of Minerva spread its massive wings.

Stripped off into a trail of dark fire the owl spoke:
Then I noticed the windowglass had started to vibrate, floor to ceiling,

Like ripples in water. She said, "That plane is flying too low,"
"& it's flying right at us," the huge, sweeping, perfectly clear eye,

A cataract of all deadened voices at once—locked in on target:
Me, in the ghosted window-wall, acoustic decay, smoked glass.

I actually made eye contact with the man in the cockpit,
& at the last possible moment, the jet veered up 20 stories,

& the office was plunged into darkness.
When I stood back up, the air outside was full of paper.

---

29   It was just beginning to incarnate when—the dead to me a shepherd are & all
      the living want...5:46 AM, 11 Sep 2011 · 1 sec ago via the word

I was 3 feet from my cubicle. It felt like the floor
Was being pushed up into my feet.[30]

I was ripped open to the sky 70 smoking stories in the air
& stunned to see how blue it was, aching, wounded, lovely,

As slowly, gently, the building began to sway
Through the moment that had 3 hearts—

One of these had been consumed away with lightness
(Give to me a mind undarkened)—the second,

In the case of my own small ventricle
Had combined its flightlessness with a mutilated alphabet

Behind which large sapphire tears of burning jetfuel were dripping
Down an elevator shaft—(O sunwaters of yestermorrow:

At the moment the paths of the Sun Being cross:
Purify me when I'm reborn/decapitated on impact/reburn its flight

Along a bright path in essence of sight) to remember but—
I flew I through a small meaningless birth

Undarkened to the sorrowing waters below
Toward that place the living may not face

                              where she lifted a silver bowl
Fill'd with rose petals & sheep's blood to the sun
Thus to appease the Nations of the Dead:

Onely I flew in my long warbling thoughts telescoped through days,
Lit through the building a fiery gash in the deep blue screen.

---

30   Power is a word the meaning of which we do not understand. —Tolstoy 3:09
       AM, 10 Sep 2016

(& the metal owl swivels its head, blinks, stops at 10:28
On the North Tower collapse:
                  & took your hand,

                  stepped off the ledge, into air...[31]

Exhaust in my long long hair to remember that I could with the falling
Be scratched into the pavement in this fully grown child's clumsy hand

          I AM AN
          IRONWORKER
            I helld you in my hands
            I did not know who you were
              & now I am showererd clean
            but yet I still feel dirty
            I don't know why
              but I feel ashamed
            who were you

I have amniosis like the tears in God's silence.

Spread its wings only with the extinction of falling dawn
Coated with a secret radar-absorbent material: there is nothing.

Onely through extinction as from its afterlife the owl flew
Into a clockface, impregnating me in a low—

(Come with me through the old smoking military tunes)
(Tap your foot)

—in a low quiver, at belly, with its secret as of moaning,
Traveling along the ground in a blanket of asbestos & incinerated people,

Its flight began: The 'Now' is empty
                        ...to disperse into 202 soda-can sized bomblets,
causing a string of explosions...
        (Top Pentagon strategists privately acknowledge it was a mistake to make the food
ration dropped by U.S. cargo planes the same color (yellow) as cluster bombs)

---

31   Were you small then, barely connected to the ground but moving fast, away from
        the inferno, like a hologram of a moving flame? · 7:28 AM, 11 Sep 2011 · 2 minutes
        ago via web from Weymouth, MA

Or rather, the owl blinked night
with the click of a camera shudder: there.
& most of the victims were children:[32]

(In this article, we'll find out how such stealth aircraft as the B-2 and the F-117 Nighthawk
"vanish." The B-2 is a 172 foot wide flying wing, but its advanced stealth capabilities
make it seem smaller than a sparrow in radar!)

The owl's eye said
'Onely' said 'One'

In its still light. & the left eyelid translucent as always
Which suddenly & mechanically rolled its gaze

Through to the girl/in the belly of that plane
Who was still wearing a face: & the third heart

Was beating its wings inside her ribcage,
Having filled this room with my own immense, small thumping

Just at the weight of my considerable mammalian wailing,
On again, off again with the falling of dusk, dawn, dusk, is nothing

To spread its wings across the broadcast waters,
Sweep its invisible gaze through supersonic screams

Until I was simply, absurdly, *here*...

The aircraft has 2 major defenses against
radar detection. The first is the plane's ~~radar-absorbent~~ surface. The composite material
used in the bomber is specifically designed to absorb radio energy with optimum efficiency.

...in faint infrared (thermal) signatures They said
"The war is on" in faint, spectral murmurs:

The second element to radar invis
bility is the plane's shape. Radar waves bounce off the planes in the same way light bounces
off a mirror. A flat vertical mirror will bounce your image straight back at you—you'll see
yourself.

A dark mass of contagion in the owl's pupil

---

32   "Being in the Taliban is like wearing a jacket of fire" · 9:36 PM, 16 Nov 2013 ·
      2 minutes ago via web from Weymouth, MA

But if you tilt the mirror 45 degrees, it will reflect your image straight upward. You won't see ~~yourself~~, you'll see an image of the ceiling. The plane itself also works like a curved mirror. & the bombs don't have to see anything at all to find their way to the target! (See How Smart Bombs Work for more information.)

& the sky spread with planes

>   *...Unmanned Aerial Vehicles orbited for hours above the desert battlefields, feeding the locations of targets to stealth aircraft circling overhead, calling down a massive, concentrated JDAM[33]...*

>   (It guides free-fall bombs in any weather using an intertial navigational system & a global positioning system—just like the one in your own car—located in the tail)

Behind which each face was merely incinerated
Once the O$_2$ in the lungs had been replaced with fire

Say swift: say gathering in its movement:
Each moment consumes it self

>   (from wide-ranging altitudes in straight & level flight or by diving)

Right through to the heartbeat
Onely decay of the aura in motion I flew

>   (like smart cluster bombs, the JDAMN merely adds a satellite-based guidance system to "dumb" bombs—the Pentagon prefers the term "gravity" bombs—as large as 2,000 pounds)

My face cupped in quotation marks of aphasia,

>   It having been dreamed to me by echolocation
That my heart be flapped in oil (Coded as scream)

& all dimensions collapsed their gaze as the crosshairs zeroed in on target,

---

33   Specifications of U.S. 'JDAM' Bomb: A primer on the satellite-guided bomb system called Joint Direct Attack Munition: JDAM is an air-to-surface weapon · 5:46 AM, 16 Nov 2013 · 3 minutes ago via web from Weymouth, MA
Contractor: Boeing & Nothingness Corp.
Length: 119.5 inches to 152.7 inches
Weight: 1,013 pounds to 2,115 pounds
Wingspan: 19.6 inches to 25 inches
Range: 15 miles
Ceiling: 45,000-plus feet
Cost: $21,000 per tailkit
Projected Inventory: 87,496 total – 62,000 Airforce and 25,496 Navy

A grey building that looked like a hospital or a ministry

& I followed the action right until that baby hit its target
& all at once my television screen was filled with static...

Some of them wore screams Those who still had bodies:
Some, whose echoes had been reduced to ash, wore bending air,

Prismatic fringes, inhuman flux, light
Of this thinking substance (Revive the fire) & flew

Who perished lightly above the waves—owl, beat, we,
I am sick with fear. I could give you the sound of its wings

If I knew its wings: "Oh. Oh no." Its flight in search of the inner pulse.
If I were speaking the fire language in a coarse grain of flying,

If the consumed light hadn't died already in a pink nest,
In the ear future: if I had a soul,

It was speaking the incarcerated language—

'Theatre of War,' or so they called it. Take flight
From my mouth spreading your wings, owl,

In the form of black cash: Onely with the falling
(This man throws up his arms/a woman screams/fingers entangled/

Wriggling as they fall/then shrank back to dots
As the camera all of a sudden pulled back to the long view[34])

Of the I swallowing into dawn into a cosmic brain lesion
Of the Birdless Aorta

There is nothing to remember but

---

34   #PurestOfHolyFires Cut to 3rd face: "My entire body was burning like crazy.
      We've come to hate the skies" · Sun Sep 11 2011 5:46:40 (CDT) via web from
      Framingham, MA

Little Domesday Clock
Stroke the Third: Stripper & Suicide Vest

—but wait: you there, standing in the arcades,
(Grand Central, Grand Whatever)
bending away between 2 mirrors that face each other
at Macy's, say, or a gentleman's club: You, an embolism,
just waiting to explode: *tick, tick, tick,*
strapped behind the pink dome of the frontal plate
to ride that mirror-curve back up the bloodstream to God, (or wherever)
where you'll go off: You, you & you
are the messenger particle.
Just when you thought the people would go on walking by forever,
or standing there asleep on their feet,
frozen in a swarm around you—& please your honor[35],
finger on the switch: big, weeping, black gasoline eyes
that go all the way back to the epicenter in a single charge,
this massive inverted gasp, this explosion on pause, this
whispered word: *boom*
Shall truly listen to the People as they wake, all at once.
That's right. Adorable. Perfect. Alive…We the…
(We the Collapsed, We the Exploded) the PPL
who mewl kittenishly & whimper & howl all the way right up to the end,
shall be lifted, soon, (*tick, tick*) in the Grand Blowback
(in the Great Collapse) shall stay woke…
& meanwhile: you there,
in the van, we"ll call you Customer X.
Go on watching her. We'll call her Crystal, the dancer, La Scanta
as she fills up her boyfriend's Ducati at the Exxon station
across the parking lot from work, wearing somethin' tight.
All of us are hanging down in the same damn hanging glacier.
All of us dead & living combined.
& when it falls into the Arctic Sea, you, finger
on the hair-trigger: you, in the shag-carpeted interior,
watching her: & you, Crystal, the exotic dancer,

---

35   I shall carry your crossed-out eyes in me like a black bar in the moonlight because
        I write for myself & the dead · Sun. 19 Sep 2010 23:39:46 (CDT) via web from
        Framingham, MA

wearing something lacy & black & maddeningly tight, holding the nozzle,
finger on the trigger, fumes, cellie, muaaaa![36]
Music's still flashin' me, fire still liftin' me, higher, higher,
lovely head cocked to the sky in blond downward streaks sparkling. See,
the people are the dangerous part of the iceberg, meltingly so.
Jagged & brief, glittering & black & long: in a blast...
Or up the plastic tubes we go, inching ever so slowly,
in brightly colored liquids ("Look Bobby," you said just this morning,
Crystal, "it's like Lifesavers!") in the ward for kids, because yesterday
he got a burn where the chemicals leaked out of the tube
onto the inside of the back of his hand, & it won't ever go away, so today
he gets as many lollipops as he wants.) Or: down,
down the disrupted Gulf Streams we go,
spilled in fire-whispers, in migrations, in child soldiers, waves of refugees,
eroded coastlines, new seas for all I know, tons of plastics,
drought, floods, wildfire...& just like that,
we're parted alright, like Pharoah's army (but unsmothered)
(unmothered), exactly as the sky shall be parted,
but tight as a tick full of blood when it comes unseeable,
above the IGA at dusk, & it will come, split sapphire
from blazing peach, at the Endzone Gentleman's Club,
(backdrop: a small buzz from the busted neon sign, crackling
with each jump)—Hallelujah!—a woman's curved form
in long luminous gas-discharge tubes lighting up the night. & you,
Crystal, (watching the watcher from the van)
for this particular species & tint of gasping in the gloaming
goes seizing its way on back in a slow implosion, invisibly,
all the way back in this lapsed detonation,
from this moment all the way back in a flash to the summer
Mama used to bring you here each day, knee-high to a barstool,
to pick wild asparagus, & then, after,
the summer little Kiley disappeared onto the milk cartons,
before her stepdaddy brought her back,
all of it played back in a reverse gasp of slow combustion.

---

36   Imagine showing the American ghetto to an android programmed to see beauty &
      understand love · 5:57 PM, 11 Nov 2013 via web from Framingham, MA

Six nights a week you return to this parking lot
like a winter finch in an irruption year,
                              diesel fumes, razzle-dazzle, booze,
burning asphalt where a virgin meadow used to grow.
There were softer acts of God, too:
mama's hand wrapped around your wrist for instance, right here,
as she showed you how to pull out the entire plant whole
by the white roots—a man's stubble against your ass, years later—
the scar from the C-section—that was little Bobby—& yesterday, you,
sliding down that silver pole from heaven, from, ha,
the dayglo ceiling stars—& BOOM!
Boom! shakalakalaka Boom! shakalakalaka, Boom! shakalakalaka,
Boom. We the Watchers have been filled
in advance with all of this. & when we're parted & alone,
we'll each of us explode, We the _____ :
(just watch me now): bright exfoliations, black prisons,
sea-ice collapsing *oh yeah*, migration triggers, warm beer,
vendors, Marlboro Reds, scanté, the kids,
bitches in heat, black cash, fumes, in days, nights: & humbly
all of us blasted out of all our head,
we shall offer our pure products to the sky:
Viagra of course. A suicide vest. Us. US.
Large breasted Xtian women looking wholesome & slutty.
Gay shirtless skiing trip. All of it played back in that exploding paused:
Semtex, Markie Mark's underwear, Da sein, Boo-té,
Maximum Penis Growth, "Blue blue window behind the stars,"
& so on. Because, just because—the people
Dance it all away in a held breath!
Sublime & mighty name![37]
BOOM! (whisper it all away in a breath: We.

The People, PPL…

---

[37]   Only in the mood of the sublime can we truly see. & it lifts the burden of the world
         · 8:15 PM, 25 Oct 2013 via web from Weymouth, MA

Seven Tweets From the Seraphs

As Mohammed said to the suicide bomber in Paradise: Holy Shi'ite! Oh snap! & the bomber responded: At least I'm not a *piece* of Shi'ite anymore[38] · 1:51 PM, 8 Sep 13 via web · Embed this Tweet

@sambrownwitt: You who tweet tweet against the dying of the pixelated light from the thick oily eye of the super-hurricane. & a storm is comin' · 10:26 PM, 14 Sep 13 via the music of the spheres via tesla coils · Embed this Tweet

Quietly, from the source of Job's wind, a newborn's hand unfolds like the Aluetian shield-fern: which, naturally, is endangered · 10:53 PM, 14 Sep 13 via the carbon · Embed this Tweet

That's how we visit: ichor in the veins, missing arms of a goddess, the Higgs-field, in the thoughts of Lazarus—Dodos, Black Rhino, the lips of Husayn Ibn Ali's severed head, Judas, the kiss · 11:57 PM, 14 Sep 13 via the blood · Embed this Tweet

For there's ever onely one reader as if every point & particle was made of sunbeams · 11:04 PM, 14 Sep 13 via the carbon · Embed this Tweet

Each one had 6 wings: with 2 he covered his face, with 2 he covered his feet, with 2 he flew, & Passenger Pigeons darkened the sky · 10:50 PM, 14 Sep 13 via the word · Embed this Tweet

& from the epicenter of the blast, one of the seraphim flew to me, having in his hand a live coal. & he touched my mouth with it. Particle: Send me Lord · 10:48 PM, 14 Sep 13 via the fires · Embed this Tweet

---

[38]   Which raises questions. You think your body is returned to you when you die? You really think we're made whole? · 10:26 PM, 14 Sep 2013 via the live coal pressed to the prophet's lips

Little Domesday Clock
Stroke the Fourth: Azimuth to Epicenter to the Finish Line

[There was a brightness attached to everything ICYMI
@the_Youngest_Day #ShelterInPlace][Feed me to the dead, yo]
[*One bright morning*][in selfies][Consider yourself fed, kiddo]
[in Gatorade© & ghostlimbs][*when this world is over*]
                    [in chips of glacial ice]
[I too #FLASH was parted from the dead][all Red Sea like]
[#POP][was melted in concussive reports][#POP]
                    [& bloody]
[I too stood @The_Finish_Line][*away oh glory*]
                    [@The_Dead_in_hoodies]
[*just a few more weary days*][*when I die*][*Hallelujah by & by*]—

[This is the youngest victim of the Boston Marathon Bombing]["No
more hurting people. Peace."][OH "That kid was 8 yrs. Old"][OH
"When I pirouette onto my new leg—"][OH "Just 4 more steps, 3
more, 2, go, you got it, come on girl, 1 more, just 1—"]

[@thefirstsyllable of the beginning of the end, @Boston, @Bismallah,
semtext in a white cap, flash the CCTV a smile @theEpicenter[39]—]
[& WEE! shall be released *bye & bye*, with the ice caps Lord]
                    [Shall overspill, yeah,
the dead sea ice in our veins in a long, low dive through the renters,
white killer whale flash@Watertown breaching, TL @Halfatimes]
                    [OH "no"]
[@every_second_the_glaciers_weep][*that bright land* إن شاء الله
                    to which I go]

---

39   @Love.in.the.time.of.drones The streets of Boston haven't been this empty
        since the blockade of Boston Harbor · 11:08 AM, 5 Nov 2013 via web

Seven Tweets From the Dead

That's what it's like to be extinguished inside of each moment, the Mockingbirds & Nightingales sing in a relentless mathematics of satisfaction & grief · 10:42 PM Sep 19th via web from Framingham, MA · Embed this Tweet

Across skyfuls of liquid sapphire with a woman's form in it, the people evade their very own lives[40] · Wed Sep 22 2010 10:53:01 (CDT) via web· Embed this Tweet

Her head falls with a spark to my shoulder afterwards, then rests beside me on the pillow · 3:25 PM Sep 18th · Embed this Tweet

For the wind is one massive prerecorded sigh & the sky, my love, a neverending brainzap · Sun Sep 19 2010 23:39:46 (CDT) via web from Framingham, MA · Embed this Tweet

In the direction of the hospital, toward which even the clouds reflected in your eyes tumble & all the kitchens drain to the same death commercial · 4:38 PM Sep 19th via web· Embed this Tweet

On the East Coast of the Middle Passage you lift my death to your ear like a conch shell & listen to the tide · 5/18/13, 22:05 · Embed this Tweet

Time is...Time is come...Tell all the clocks to stop · 10:28 PM, 19 Jul 13 (CDT) via web · Embed this Tweet

---

40   I feel blown open all over again like when you were born · 8:56 PM Sep 23rd
      via web from Weymouth, MA

Thermal Signatures

That time of night.
Gestate my spoons, Mother, your tiny foot-echoes.
For my life runs out as the gods have spun it.
Down a tree-veined, Babylonial avenue,
I cultivate my hunger: Silvertined. Tungsten. Ruptured boxspring.
Cowtongue. Lightbulb. Tungsten coil.   A gull's leg clamped in the lid
of a dumpster.
Slides down the inside when you lift it:
O my mother, be still here in my arms
Ammoniac—   Sips the pissodor of my fear:
your foot-echoes follow me through an alley
soft as the hands of mist, & carry out pure hecatombs.[41]
I want to be free of the place of hands
like all the evenings that never came.
From my crown to below my feet
Whywhywhywhy stitched to the frontaleo O in each ventricle dissolving,
"Let me but taste black blood, I shall speak true,"
Cries through the throat of a city owl
from one, from one in my step toward the ocean's edge...
A babygasp released in the radiator.
Moments ago, hours, weeks upon seconds heaped ago
& the sprinklers click waswaswaswaswas.
Have closed a hinge around each small gasp, Beloved Hunger, I walk,
a hidden chine of forbidden meat stitched to my nape
whose taste murmurs into bed: '...begat mother, begat father, begat mother...'
through the meat packing district, toward the docks,
Magnolia blossoms decity the numberless dead in a crucifodor.
We are the children of waste. The city sleeps in its glass box of injuries.
Everywhere we go we leave something behind.   Exhaust pipe.
Desolate waters. Salt.
A stopwatch sewn into my spleen.   By the river of forlorn combustion.
Tenterly you blew through me, Mother,   whose forbidden tongue I taste,
(hold one another, touch with love, & taste salt tears.)

---

41   This huge man-made hive sculpture is controlled by bees activity: http://www.slate.
        com/blogs/the_eye/2016/06/20/the_hive_by_wolfgang_buttress_at_kew_gardens_
        is_a_man_made_structure_controlled . html?worse sh_all_mob_tw_bot...via @'s
        late · 5:21 PM, 25 Jun 2016

I tremble to take a step from its 1st, I lyst from one,
from one I call: "Stole a watch, sold a watch[42]" *Tick, Tick*
past the polyhooded, toothless one moving to sip the black,
with quarters in her ears, who whispered
"Tholed it. Honey, I can't eat that thtuff. Pleathe."
O breeze, unsalt: "Go on back to your own kine."
Traded 3 livers for safe passage.
But the silken beeves of Helios were dead.
I felt it in the green nub at my heel as I walk,
the hook from which I was hung upside down at birth, there,
my body sprinkled in seawater, thole pins
looped in a cage around my heart: soft as the hand of mist.
Dis peopled & raw   dis purred even to the fledge of omb,
under the shellacked heavens, for the sea is peopled now.
I was delivered in the shape of slaughter, Mother, in after images
of used-up men, exhaust smoking, & called out sorrowfully:
I'd have gladly given the gold out of my teeth, Sirad,
Monend, Modor, Dioxad bodied through my nose,
DISEASE spraypainted on the wall of a coldhouse
where carcasses of cattle cast their shadows across the opaque windows
lit from within as they swing past on a circular trolley of hooks inside.
Trine my metals yes insatiably my tines of happiness
at the chining of the hour as I walk past
without a mur-mur, "Is this the face that burned?
Child, how could you cross over alive into this gloom?
The sea logs? The burning ships?
In the tonsured head of a soul fishing off the dock?" Yes.
Because great currents run between us, hidden barges
carry our garbage up & down these shores.
Trembles with eyes closed standing: one day mother,
machinework, goldtasted, contagionbody,
slanted wooden steps deflight into the water.
Fallen into her gaze from foot to intestinal foot.
Cirriped sky of its cabled reflection.
One day we shall have surfaced, head-foot,
whistling through your molar, MAtuH,
cutting across your teeth like a cold wind

---

42   Fifty thousand dollar watches are the pacemakers of late capitalism ·
1:28 AM, 30 Nov 2013

All too human in the Shroud of Méh t r.
Surface: the torn out heart of a dogfish.
After: still beating in his palm-& thus
was my afterbread sweet, thus
that I might throb still
against the red wall of my question
To be free & now

All our cities face west[43]

---

43   I bit my lip, rising perplexed w/ longing to embrace her. & tried 3 times putting my
arms around her—but she went sifting through my hands, impalpable, as shadows
are · 1:29 AM, 30 Nov 2013

These Pages Have Been Redacted

The Secretary Of War (2)
From the Life of the Pharaohs

The execution of this prayer will take place ~~in the desert~~
Hallelujah!
From thousands of miles away, ye gods, in a desert city, O gods,
their vanished faces be smeared [~~redacted in green night-vision~~]
along this document visible only in the dark,
written in that same aluminum explosive powder
that replaced the air in their lungs,
in their children's lungs, O gods, gods...
In terms of strength, there's a higher father I appeal to—
through their lungs, with fire.
~~Between the Steel & Gold rivers, height 2000 meters, in the green zone~~
~~of our refuge, Region of [...redacted portion...]~~
a buried bunker temple, I get great sustenance from the underground oasis.
There is a higher father [appeal to a power]
                                        One who does not speak.
White lips, rivers of moonlight in the smoke,
tiny purple fingers clutching cannisters,
dead combustion in the sand. Drink in the fire.
Breath in the faces of today's dead soldiers
blacked-out by Clear Channel, in which
we can all see those smiles, but only *you* can see what's behind them.
Through the rippling fumes of the Reflecting Pool,
this message was brought to you by. . .
~~The Bechtel Family   Shell Oil~~
a last thread of smoke rising from the stump of a child's wrist
[~~...redacted portion...~~]
The golden fatted calf flashing across the screen,
I get great sustenance, O Gods, God~~———~~
Threat level: Yellow   Code: ~~Children of Smoke~~
Time: Holy Bunker Emptied
Sponsors:~~————————   The Disney Group, the Family Dollar~~
~~Corporation, the Family Family~~.
Action: Rivers of orange plastic fire the sky shall open to drop.
The sky opened alright, Madame Secretary.
Do you feel the hand of God actually guiding you?
Do you believe the hand of God guides even the precision bombs?

Will you lead us in prayer Mother Secretary?
Let us prey. That those faces empty the mirror.
That Our sleep be emptied without dreams this daily bread. That there
be flies crawling on their eyeballs, in the region of
[~~...redacted portion...~~]——————the eyeballs guy promised it,
Forgive us this day.
                    [I turned in the President's sleep & the
Secretary blacked out my mind
~~with a fat magic marker]~~
That the veil covering the socket in my chest uplifted be.
Behind which the starcarcass sleeps. For we are from the Reality Bomb
    community.
Black bars over the eyes. Fat black stripes across the type. That You
pass Your hand through my ribcage, Lord.
Lift my heart in its prayercloth——— ~~I keep a child's severed hand there,~~
that You wipe my heart clean away of the nuclear fingerprint.
That a white wind blow their faces through the sleeper cells of my
    heart,
through the bunker, where I can feel those tiny fingers stir.
Let my heart be whole.
The Secretary murmured through my throat: ~~"Heart?~~
~~Its crushed, velvet hinges are little more than fluid,"~~ —
& escaped her thin white prayerducts.
"Amen: in the event of dirty bomb,
chamber will empty of stars & POW
your body is a pyramid suit ——— ~~of dark pure particle waves~~
into God's empty empty face."

Two
Frankenstein[44];
Or, The Presence Chamber

~

Γνωθ ι Σεαυτου
Know Yourself

~

"War is the art of conquering *at home*."
— THOMAS PAINE, *The Rights of Man*

---

44   Thank you for forgiving my spatial, temporal, physical, emotional, intellectual, cultural Dis functions · 4:41 PM, 7 Jan 2014

Little Domesday Clock
Stroke the Fifth: Time & Tide Waits for No

—& c: & see: & She: & seize: as in:
the gray-eye'd dying seas are rising, We the Eroding, in fact,

We the Corrosive shall wear those rising sea-levels
in bleached coral, in acid wash, away. We the Pb

are going out with the tide.   Coming right back in.
          Are breaking on the slack on high water[45], We the Hordes.

Naturally, every day, We (the PPL) die of thirst, asthma, diabetes,

Your Worship, but slow of course, of hunger & fast, storm, war.
Your Refugee, M'childsoldier. See: We (of simply being born)

Particulate lung damage, the cupped palms are bearing it up,
          a desiccated surf holding lungfuls of salt & cement are,

(O my heart on fire O my eyes, Mlud)
are a bioluminescence the people produce in the Big Dance

(but only in *here*)[taps right temple] You can hear the kill cry
sometimes, as we drop out of the sky at sunfall,

magnified by pollution, in a brief biochemical galaxy
we light up in the brain & beloved—no, we flourish,

more like a massive plunge in air pressure, Mluv,
          convulsions in the stormheads, Mlud,

We descends. Every day the people, in a toddler's babble, in drone strikes,
dive down deep into the deep graveyard grass, & baby,
we sleep; we dance; *sell* it; *sell* it

---

45   O my people spread your petroleum-saturated wings · 9:01 PM, Sep 23rd via
        web from Weymouth, MA

(O untangle the knots) ————The brain flourishes
        its dendritic arbors & lights up in an Xmas tree:

(O unbeing this electrochemical storm I am O)
        am the enemy of the squid (& lóve you) & still,

still we wade into the surf of a dying ocean: a visitation true:
        a tomb: an invisible plume (God's gonna trouble the   )

when Columbus sailed the oceans new (————trouble the waves too)
to be dying————————————almost docile now, we, we, we

we^2…beasts in a charm…a protein folding/unfolding
        in replication machinery, snip, snip,

equinoctial storm a'brewin'…in swarms of us…identical, dis-
ambiguated, dis articulated, & raw: Dis

peopled, the people turn on a dime, on the virus assembly line,
        on the stalk of a white leaf, on an RNA enzyme.

Turn off the 80% of us that's water.   Turn us on
into a new protocol: X marks the spot   (Destroy the instruments,

astrolabes & sextants & such) an X-ray of bloodflow
in the lungs, a tumor-spider, Navigator[46], coastlines, a hard knot

feeding on the internal carotid, Mothergod,
        they found just a shadow on my left lung, *just*

---

46   Catastrophe Icon: When enough Monarch butterflies take flight, they can
        entirely obscure parts of the forest in what looks like orange clouds: http://
        news.national_geographic.com/news/2014/10/14101)monarch_butterfly_
        migration_threatened_plan · 1:41 AM, 27 Aug 2015

a whisper *isper*   We the Clouds have been seeded thereof.
& the droughts go on & on, heh-heh, & the wildfires, floods,

go, in exploded oil rigs collapsing into the Gulf, hee-hee,
in jellyfish, now that we're killing off the Giant Sea Turtle: We

(O my lungs & liver O my burning limbs) the People,
          in pink ears grown & harvested (listen to me)

on the backs of pink lab rats bald: We, a camera
implanted in the left eyesocket: we, a transistor coil

into the frontal lobe ingrown, We the Mortgaged to the hilt
& we, & we, in vibrato, O zoom, O snap, lapdancing in

on the singularity but not yet,   Mlud[47]—

---

47   Is it spilled ink—or white space—that makes us sing, sputtering like a cheap pen?
          Is it silence that awards power? · 8:24 PM, 25 Aug 2013

Thermal Signatures

Hundreds of unfeathered

limbs we worn *in* together—

one : un : We@the_moment

of my unfathered squall

fall all orn one der un

der: we enter the eastmarks

a hecatomb omb collapsing down

we fall to your hungry ear

all belisten me into bereathing

Your hair shone easterly just now

out of the mouth of this shirt of gnats

softly it has wailed me to the bed

soaked me of this dred-

our : has absorbed me beyond

the hour the zero hero ero s ear

Has orbed me to the dead : Darkflower : Ark

nailed my heart electrified : Moving

Portal : into the Corpse of a Great Auk[48]

Calathroat : a dark egg

has inhaloed me to this threshing floor

Disquall my frolicking brain

& the skies darkened

with Passenger pigeons for days

Clusters of Monarch butterflies bringing down

entire branches: a Corpse Flower unfolding

on time-lapse in your eyes at noomb to

morrow : a tender breeze belist

me into the bamboo garden below

Snapshot this interior of our lungs overlapping

O list list & illombinate the ruins

this exquisite animal form this

electroskeletal fern : this exoskeletal brain

---

48   Would that we were cruelty-free products in the end · 2:19 PM, 20 Dec 2013

splashed into visible seconds in the air

        this lightning for which the hamza

ach : d'Aukmothered : dismothered : stands

        mammal me arkbesmothered

Spread the shade of extinct wings[49]

        ma : between us : combine in two

Ur breathing eathing bath

        a sudden thrush of swallows

shake the branches outside as

        Ghostwings brush the window panes

Seas of waslessness echo in your ear

        rush : hush : us

I took that soft shell into my mouth

        the pink lobe of your ear: its small

unfathered bare air into

        fathéd like a panda filling its tummy

with bamboo shoots : eathed

        we was uz us eartombed there ere

pieces of coppery light conduct

        our glowing through these white sheets

To the concourse or meeting of their small motes

        Raise me a birthmark : Erthe mark

between our eyes *which they call Motors*

        where the empty hells meet

at a thighslap of shells inpinked

        & be & be : Chrysosperme : a bell

Toll the canthic fold of us : a spine : a crise

        a crisis : a cry : this way turned

that way urned electric a fern-fossil

        that way tuned epicanthic : anthic

Chrysostomos : untongued : lunged

        runed to a visible intwongue

to this hour intombed

---

[49]   Nearly Half of America's Beehives Died Last Year. All 13 Colonies of Collapse: http://munchies.vice.com/en/articles/nearly_half_of_America's_beehives_ died_last_year... · 8:09 PM, 17 May 2016

                                 Lift us Thulé all rushing down bed-inward
all seaspawn & seawrack

                                 signatures of all things I am here to read
all wings all ings all I am here to eat

                                 at the twomb of our movinglymphwing
@Genesislap : just there: there:

                                 a pink sap: a slap at 2 beyond 2 beyond
this place where the pink eyelid

                                 hasssssssssssss exploded[50]

---

50   The world BTW is one explosion outgoing. Everybody's dying & everybody's being
born, all at the same time · 11:36 PM, 24 Dec 2013

Little Domesday Clock
Stroke the Sixth: Poet of Underwater Cities

Unlock this secret for good.   The truth you say? It's coming,
with this devouring green, it's in the post, this vour, this dower, this down:
coastal cities underwater, holy appetite. Our thirst was the key, our hunger.
The truth: strike me from the record. <the drone strike is coming>
Really? *Really?*   This We?   Like: We're-not-going-anywhere-

but-down, with our end-y-days appetite? The People, cuh, people,
swarming schools of Asian carp, waves of refugees, payrolls, fluid borders,
mass extinctions, extinct verbs,   are the hordes on each Black Friday...
In the darkly shining uranium mills, in finely pulverized sand, We the PPL
are gonna sleep pretty much forever, PLS, or not at all, <life/life>

with our long ass half-lives <if/if> our viruses, our styrofoam.
"If somebody wants to rapture me up," <my mind has been set free>
Michael said, in the wine store, on Market Street, "that'd be just fine with me."
See: The People, people,   irradiated in the tailings, they die,
Cast in orange dayglo capes washing across the overburden,

in a thread of repossessions, bundled subprime mortgages
<she used to call you 'my little bundle of joy'><the butterfly screamed out
the thick eye of the cyclone>   in one collateralized debt obligation
<one hurricane after another>   blink after oily blink &...out.
What happens when nobody dies? <Do we metastasize our loss?>

In the world of the ten thousand year per tick Atomic Clock?
10,000 years per toxic asset,   per stroke?
In the World of the Ten Thousand Cheap Plastic Things?
We the People,   the people, people, are buried under a mountain
<are/were/are> just dying to explode.[51]

---

51   One thought fills immensity: It's a mad mad mad chemical world: BBC News
       Emmissions of CO$_2$ driving rapid oceans 'acid trip'_http://www.bbc.com/news/sci-
       ence-environment-24904143 · 11:52 AM, 17 Dec 2013

<we^4/we^5/we^6/we^7> Gone.   The first breeze of success

delivered on short credit. & poof! Milkweed pods burst open.
White feathers.   On the scatter.   But we're not. Gone, that is? Drifting?
Like a radiated plume over the Ukraine? A seeded cloud? Spent cesium,
carbon of course, methane sky pixels, cold liquid cash disappeared
into 1's & 0's. Are we?   The horde?   On white horse?

Riots, gossip, flash mobs, depleted food stores,
fissile isotope U-235 & the depleted uranium, the yellowcake
Left Behind <that's us>   <all because we forgot to code switch>
<read: history><read: a brand new coastline carved out>
<decode the synapse>   <all because the unburned hydrocarbons in the sky>
<burn><urn><rn>   <had been torched after all>

<all b/c we touched Her massive empty face at last^{52}>
        </& you & you & you//>

---

52   Even as the spinners spun for him the day his mother bore him. #Odyssey •
      9:00 AM, 21 Jul 2016

Thermal   Signatures

5, 5 to the number of my forefinger
a shining glass bowl
an orchid-bloom floating on the water
this instant: Golden number 5: Epact 13
5 to this very attosecond's Easter[53]
When I touch this floating bloom
& it has upblushed me down, 3, 2
I speak into the absolute aerie,
in a pool of platinum Sundecay
Dis second, this hemocide
What then the golden number to this day
from the blind lean of the sun
Liquidpup: Vessel: upupupupup
Form of…falling water through my cide
deep into my paralysisbloom
Float the ghost-weft of a womb
& never so much as today
have I turned so heartscalded
that has so shed me into enormous sound
a 5 throated s-s-sect of gold on
Ah, slumberthumb, I ecco-rise
this Fridaywater having so unblushed me
These crawling seconds unbloom me
it casts me inside out through my cide
at glass on the windowpane
missing a ling, through the ides
to the Mecca missing pastward listing a way
Flashed bronze on the whitewash
dried stickystreams of Hemo
defleshed to unseem this vandal
Après moi, to the Word:
Undecay: an unsearching, a deluge unlocking
Efflorescent scum: upreach its echostreams
Screaming through my bronzed side & I
Now:

between these loose racemes, 5, 5:
to the Metonic cycle of my woumbnd
5 white petals connect to this thumbstalk
Dominical letter C: Ctide: the S of C
5: by my silvered tongue, my crown.
first one, then another, 5, 4,
that my forethroat be peaced of gold,
into the solute artery-bloom,
which has upshed me through
this bruised pullwater, years of Eastertide:
inside this severed instant. I sect blindly
into my own warm oombwater
Ape: Every day a new god arrived
Shape: Downrisen to these white cruCipetals
that looms the purplinguptinge.
through this tracheal carapace, *this* fast.
has this place so abandoned me, *on palsy*,
on a tracheal stalkend of accidence that,
the movement of 5 petaleyes in the room
on a spanglepatter that coindances the floor.
through the mask of my Unday,
b-b-baby flies at grass, at glass.
Zounds! that I trach these quiverings
a circle bissected to my marsupial grace
I too bow Eastward,
at the moment my shadow shall reach
I braise my twongue & rise & shout
first this white flower in hand, then these
unfurling purple like a rip in the air, white,
it shall upreach me having risen,
to the coming ward: a hungerecho:
the goldend: the sunmarked Now: the flood
Now: dis-sever the first & last day[54]
finger the gash, ahhh*shhhhh*…
to the Ark

---

53   I will take whatever grace I'm offered: in '89, the last golden toad went out quietly, disappeared like an Oxford comma, a coma brain…only to be replaced by the "Golden totes" · 5:08 PM, 22 Sep 2011

54   Thus the ancients spoke of destiny: Saltwater fish extinction seen by 2048 http://t.co/QFkAd8IIA4 · 5:09 PM, 22 Sep 2012

Little Domesday Clock
Stroke the Seventh: The Drone Inside (Syria, Iraq, Yemen, 2014)

& the sky jumped like neon, one tiny synaptic burst
after another O my people, in baby tongues—*tick/tick*—in ice tongues,
Your Honor, Your Worship, Your Grace,   & you, & you

& you, in nucleotides & beige jumpsuits,
in the small ivory figures of detainees at Camp X-Ray, seen from above,
moved around in outdoor cages, cowled in orange: we are just *nowhere.*

Are one massive human wave folding down[55]: are
(altogether now) at prayer (/amen!) painted in the strobelight, bound,
blindfolded in sight goggles, ears plugged, white noise, Ted Nugent, froth.

Testify. *Sell* it, baby. Brang it—the word, that is—back & forth
the people rocked, lips moving in prayer, Sell *it.* But on the inside,
you were filled with that high-pitched piercing scream

exactly like the sound in a department store, (unbound)
the one you can only hear when you've been there all day, at work,
(Active ingredients: larvicides, organochlorides, pyrethroids,

non-target species, longbow hellfire, AGM 114 N,
metal augmented charge), exactly like the high-pitched screaming
of that hornet your cousin sprayed in Raid one summer & for 5 full minutes,

you swore you could actually *hear* it scream as it writhed.
That's how the people screamed, quietly, on the inside, in drones
the size of dragonflies, in cashpoints, at the epicenter of the explosion,

in waterboarding, in blast charges, in Hellfire missiles...

---

55   Inside this monstrous deep learning system: Slash n' burn the panting brain:
        Amazon is the new Amazon · 3:27 PM, 15 Nov 2013

Little Domesday Clock
Stroke the Eighth: The Timepiece & the White Whale

From here on out, the people shall be...
a life-sized map of ourselves...of the oceans, dying, a massive tomb:
a dark mass on the brainscan, & you & you & you...

& those oceans within, your very own dead zone shall be: you & yours.
Size of...Texas, jellyfish clustered at the tethers of an off-shore oil rig,
shall be, shall be...form of: a sperm whale quattrocento

washed up on the coast of Holland,
30 feet of plastic agricultural covering in its gut, & you, & you—
may the felled Redwoods rise through your sleep

for a thousand years & more, a curse.
May the Golden-cheeked warbler haunt you with its lispy *zee zoo*
until it's gone. I hope it tortures you to madness *zeebezee,*

see: walk off the planet into the parking lot sunset in cowboy boots,
polyester checked shirts, alone or in pairs, a virgin forest paved over,
another promise gone, just like that   (& you, & you)

for the people were a dark virgin once, too.
& now we're a sequence, a growth, a viral genome replication
& you & you: shall be: shall be a hymn[56]

a replicant & you ——————a can't, a replican-do,
zeebeezee, a synchronous brief of moonlight, zee zoo, on the tidal pool
where it all began: a delitescence, (the people)

a secret, (people): a sign, a morpheme, & you,
you: past tense allomorph, sun sinking fast & faster
than father's fat gold pocket watch sank. & sunk. & sinks still.

---

56   Commercial break: It's all about breaking this hold that death has on all of
       us, which is why I always coat my life in Pam · 7:40 PM, 19 May 2013

& still it ticks at the bottom of the sea: & - & - & still
it's about to burst like a drunkard's heart, at midnight, (gin's gone)
just where you dropped it that afternoon, buried in the sandbed,

& still it ticks now silted from all points at once:
from inside the whale's stomach, through your very own
heart-valve, through your pulse, all points south,

just as it filled your sleep—swarms of people darkening
all summer long, remember? With static? White noise?
& it fills your chambers even now, white sound, cis, cis

cissing, my sister, your heart wrapped in cotton,
chiming out the first few bars of *A Mighty Fortress Was Our Lord,*
chipping away at you, at the quarter hour,

still striking away at your tiny 13 yr. old bell,
in that 13 yr. old sleep, a deliquescence: once, once & once,
in raw tonnages of carbon, a quiescence,

in waves of refugees, in new coastlines, erosions,
even a brand new ocean, yes, at full fathom, once upon *an inflation,*
& you were still growing, yes & you

& you, still growing in tropospheres, growing small,
in computing power, in millstones around the neck,
in chime after chime twisted into the fat heart

of the white whale until it bursts
& the sky shall crack—somebody gimme an Amen—
it's a beautiful day, welcome to the world, sunrise, sunset,

welcome to the aching world, a singular sapphire drop
miraculously formed—& in the endless black matter
the sun shall expand in that first massive pulse

of the Special Paymaster's mind—[57]

---

[57]   Has darkness met your expectations? Does it spin like a centrifugue · Sun Sep
19 2010 22:19:19 (CDT) via web from Framingham, MA

Ten Tweets From the Future

Which is why, in morning coat & black dress, the people were a xerox of the toxic ocean, long before we breathed out just once in our sleep (& like that) we were gone · Sun Sep 19 2010 23:39:58 (CDT) via web from Framingham, MA · Embed this Tweet

The people carried their toxic assets to bed with them · Sun Sep 19 2010 23:34:28 (CDT) via web from Framingham, MA · Embed this Tweet

& the moonlight was searching the tunnels of a mare's eye & glaciers collapsed under a deluge of 80 odd billion plastic bottles per year après moi · Sun Sep 19 2010 17:39:48 (CDT) via web · Embed this Tweet

When people speak a futureless language, they put the future on equal footing with the present: Après moi le déluge · 1:09 AM - 27 Sep 13 (CDT) via web · Embed this Tweet

Like: I kind of feel like my genes need to be stopped[58] · 10:41 PM, 4 Apr 2014 · Embed this Tweet

Empty as a conch shell, pearly as the interior, white as the dead. Lifted with the white fires. Write it out: in bleached coral reefs, vanished sea-ice, in extinction · 6:13 PM, 21 Nov 13 · Embed this Tweet

Trace my thumbprint to the source: this pelican, adrift in its box of clear plastic sky: O my people, spread heavenwide your oil-coated wings · Wed Sep 22 2010 12:08:37 (CDT) via web · Embed this Tweet

---

58   For every rose a thorn: Can a rose shatter in cartoon land? Dip it in liquid nitrogen & see: Can't you bring a man back from the dead here? · 1:12 AM Sep 18th via web

Far longer than we were pregnant with our very own lives. Just toggle to the enlightened & you'll see · 2 min ago via web · Embed this Tweet

Talk about language extinction: Hey College, I got words for you: in 10 yrs I bet, nobody will use the phrase "you're welcome." They'll say "no problem." · 7:42 PM, 22 Oct 13 · Embed this Tweet

For it's been the Age of the Insect now for about 400,000,000 years[59] · 1 sec ago via web · Embed this Tweet

---

59   Do you know It's the End of the End of the World? I don't know, could you hum a few bars? · 2 sec ago via web

These Pages Have Been Redacted

The Secretary Of War (3)
From the Life of the Marionettes

There *is* a Father [redacted portion escapes subject's pink little heart]
O *wondrous* [heart redacted] dissolve lightly the Secretariat of Whispers,
[screen filled with static]———— ~~What is G d but One?~~ —

[Access code:] Where is the child with nuclear fingerprints?
[Whispers of smoke thread from the Secretary's dried tearducts]
[Brought to you by————— ~~Clear Vision~~ —]

[which a tiny immaculate flame shall emit,— ~~the Day of the Embed~~ ————]
Pulled like a fingernail from each fingertip: a stranger's footprint,
a thumbprint on the mirror, silent thump in my chest.

Sink your radiotranslucent fingers into this sacred,
plastique heart. The stars were invisible in my conception of time.
I was that thump-thump, thump-thump in my little Jesus of the Lamb,

Alpha chopper day. An apache helicopter
[onely in my chest] was whacking through the medullanean thumbprint
into which these messages [~~brought to you by The Omega~~] had been carved:

Right ventricle: ~~Let there be an opportunity for draining~~ —
Left ventricle: ~~Lest the sacred heart in razorwire be bound~~
Such as that surveilled from [~~...redacted portion...~~]

from the Life of the swathed in immaculate, soft, intelligence flames service,
O Secretary of Now: [~~this dunk in the water was brought to you by~~ ——]
Onely in nightvision scopes [~~...decapitated portion...~~ ————]

can the soaked civilian airtime be broken into the pure, beheaded binary
of a person's heart, those 1's, those 1's, those lovely seaside tunes...
Back behind the static where a bloated, golden calf flashes

across the darkened screen, I bloomed. Put your palms to it.
Filled with static whispers of light. Feel it?
Touch the screen lightly, past midnight in your flickering den,

visible rustles of light beneath the fading screen, a light shock on the palm.
Feel it? [~~...Hooded naked man, arms outspread, wires~~]
God is a real man. "Quite literally we didn't even hear an explosion.

You see the light before you hear anything. & we saw
this massive red fireball, & it literally masked an entire mountain
& we just started laughing, laughing, just out of pure joy

that we weren't on the receiving end of that—"
When the President bows his head in prayer,
with the ~~Secretary of the Disappeared in the sit room~~, jetplanes fill the sky,

drones, fire. & the helicopters rise—If your television screen
should suddenly be filled with green buildings when you wake,
it only means the Secretary has blacked out ~~your eyes~~

with her fat magic marker, has filled ~~in~~ ~~your fat little heart~~
that the prayercloth has come to cover your head in a hood;
that, at last, you can see through the green eye

at the top of the pyramid, in which the President sleeps in his bunker.
[...the real message was delivered clearly enough,
& for some, that was the point from which space-time suddenly flowed.]

~~The face in question was a mother's face~~ ~~in Minnesota, say,~~
~~at the Mall of America; or in a desert city, in the medina?~~
Among dates, bolts of fabric, ~~or here, near automotive.~~

Anyway, she screamed, that much we know, right there in prayer linens
& life baskets lined with ultra-suede, near lawn ornaments,
below-ground bunker implements, she screamed,

seeing the face of her only son melted again
as the explosively formed penetrator went off again,
concealed in a pile of trash by the road.

Her surveillance number was released
into the soothing elevator hymns above.
Burned into the abominable powdered neon light.

Pumped into that distant, high-pitched department store screaming
in a barely detectable, high-pitched buzz.   & she collapsed
~~into the underexposure of her son's face.~~

That's what happens when the President bows his head in prayer.

ONE
THE APHASIA CLOCK@DOMESDAY.OHM
A MODERN DAY PROMETHEUS[60]

~

E

~

"Signatures of all things I am here to read, seaspawn and seawrack, the nearing tide, that rusty boot. Snotgreen, bluesilver, rust: coloured signs. Limits of the diaphane. But he adds: in bodies."
— JAMES JOYCE, *Ulysses*

---

60   I have proof that God hallucinates: The World · 9:43 PM, 7 May 2016

Thermal Signatures

Omphalostone pressed to my Sheanavel...
Glitterkidney & heartsound along a seabrake of pebbles I walk.
Heere the compasse set in Longitude from the Meridian of London 58
In this place where my insides om pha are lost los to a standing wave.
Seacalf's liverheartkidneystone lifted in the froth I lift to the sun.
Omphalosignal & moving of seagulls degr.30.min. & in Lat.64.
4 or 5 of the clock of the nonne Thursday the 29 of August
To remember unto you the diurnall of our course
Crying (land) it being very likely the breaking of the sea white
Into the shape of my name: Seafroth, Amnion, Devour...
When I was an infant my father held me in one hand
By the ankles over the surf:
To dangle me Surgefallall sweet tuneful voice
From the innershrine of gullflight it sound
To dip me full bodily tasting the salt as he held me there
At 30.degr. Westward variation. Wee took the heighth.
The sunne being 5 degrees above the horizon : O : pollutionfattened
To have no better sustenance than their own urine to sustain them,
Some were sick of fluxes : Roger Large, John Mathew & many died
Whose names I knew not at the writing hereof An. Dom 1587[61]
Desiring greatly their expedition which perished almost a hundredth soules.
Ostone : osdown : its green half-lip in an underlife : Own : Halflife
Was so contagious Time went away A very mighty Porpose
With a harping yron
& brought away part of its flesh sticking upon that yron
But could recover onely that one passing thorough the Ocean
the ocean in heardes, which did portend storme.
Ocea : Os : Omphaloslakes its waste through my toes
& seacombers fall...& all pastwardnow, exhausted, all
...alos...sshhh...sshhhnow...
Wee sounded 1 while 7 fadome then 5 fadome then 4 & lesse.
Ocean, weep phalloms down, Os-slap my smooth sheacalves, sh-Sea.

---

61   "Jonathan Ferrell Is Dead. Whistling Vivaldi Wouldn't Have Saved Him" http://
www.slate.com/articles/news...via @slate. Poetry is a future history · 11:02 PM, 5
Jan 2014

Wee found shole water & smelt so sweet a smel
As if some delicate garden abounding with all kind of odiferous flower
Land could not be farre distant God be thanked.
O : marking the middle point of Earth : Wee lay one glass upon the lee.
So great a substance : Oombs my ankles : He had consumed : that
Westward I look.
Whorled into a whelkshape & heald my ear with a touch
Os s-sea tongue, consume.
Wild sea money cast to my feet : Pulled in its omphalosurge & backthirst
& the palsy shingle pulled backward shakes in place:
Omphalalos, alos, alossshsume...Westward
At the lead sun sinking into the ocean today I look.
Along the coast of Desolation wee trended & the bayes of Placentia,
The bayes of Conception which some call Trespassa.
After the miscarying of the great ship God manifestly delivered us
Having discharged our harquebuz-shot such a flocke of Cranes
With a cry as if an armie of men had showted altogether
To delight the Savage people –
Arose under us the most part white[62]
& some went on shore to play with them at the football.
As soone as they did come to strike the ball all
Our men did cast them down in feare
Sing O seanipples of stone
Caught in the backsurge
Like the Swanne that singeth
Before her Death
O...pha...lo...ossshhh...

I have bene at 73 degr. finding the sea all open.

---

62   How do you define success? African-American male respondent: "Being able to say
you're alive" 1:14 AM, 27 Sep 2013 via web

Little Domesday Clock
Stroke the Ninth: Love in the Anthropocene

For as the sentence of that strict
& terrible last account cannot be evaded—
      to the last syllable of unrecorded time

seconds before the chime, at which the oceans
shall be lifted away in a warm blanket, & you & you & you,
played back to infinity in sun-pulses, woke,

awakened, called to account, vacuumed up with all the voice data—
right down to the last extinct species, unnamed, undiscovered,
right down to the last dime.

     We shall either sleep, or be evaporated,
      We the People.

A guide to living: Households: 1 smallholder.
1 freeman. Value: Cities of pigs: Taxable value: 0.5 geld units:
a mysterious spume on all these tons of dung-(dong)

foaming up through the slats of an industrial hog farm,
4 ft. high, rainbow-sheen: my heart leaps up[63]...
Value to lord in 1066: £1 sterling. Value to lord in 1086: £0.5

Value to Lord in 2014: $$bill/tons of pigshit exploding.
Value to Lord: 385 bitcoin: a barn lifted a couple feet off the ground,
1,500 pigs instantly killed upon combustion. Value to Lord:

If the mountain will not come to Mahomet,
the mountain shall have its hat knocked off with semtex.
If the skyscraper will not come to the Boeing 767-200ER...

---

63 ...when I behold a rainbow in the sky: The pig is father to the spam http://www.
motherjones.com/tom-philpott/2013/05/menace-manure-foam-still-haunting-
huge-hog-farms · 7:20 PM 1086 (CDT) via web from Charlottesville, VA

with its 10,000 gallons of fuel, then We the Peeps:
in smartphone records, insecticides, occupations, CDOs,
phonecalls from the plane, "recycled" laptops,

bundled subprime mortgages, glowing stone tablets
& rising cancer rates: in toxic debt pools,
credit cards, pacemakers, digital scrolls: We the————

shall come to the Niger Delta without bodies,
shall come to Seelampur, our digital identities
& electronic dollars intact, baby elephants dying off, children

boiling motherboards to segregate copper.

"The telephone exchange in Varanasi
also has huge amounts of electronic scrap," he smiles.
"I'd like to get the tender for it."[64]

"My kids are naked ghosts in this pile of trash,"
until those invisible bundles spilled over into one another,
unlocked each frozen moment like sea-ice, Deity,

World-stopper, World-pulse, soft sugary yellow surface
split open, brilliant white flesh blazing inside, & you, (because
there isn't anybody else), an electric crackle, & you, & you—

—————————

—were such a strange sequence of darkling chimes,
your finger slowing the globe along the Tropic of Cancer
as it spins in chromatic sequent toil—& 1 & 1 &—stop:

right there at 0. Trace this second

with the astrolabe back to its source.
Measure this altitude-depth by its minor key, between
the buzzing bailbond sign in mid-neon jump & Thalhimers

---

64   That's why light is wasted on the people, I'm afraid · Mon Sep 20 2010
      11:01:11 (CDT) via web

boarded up inside this dispensation of 1's & 0's,
this binary flow away from a smoking coordinate we once called now,
not being-towards-death, but a glance of the eye, ecstasis.

Calculate the azimuth: blasted away

like Grandfaddy's prostate tumors, seeded
with tiny irradiated Au particles to guide the radiation,
just like a predator drone.[65] Now: blasted away

like ice-bergs for the exotic ice trade: look at yourself,
standing there in the corner mirror, unlocked in the past,
such an acute not-yet-now, years away, the no-longer-now that flows

you into almost walking into the quicksilver
of your own reflection, the angle of one mirror converged upon
by another, in Men's Fashion. & you stood there didn't you,

staring at the threshold, the back of your own head;
you almost entered your own profile staring
in stop-trance: "That guy," you thought,

"would look just like me"—black hair,
baby face, glasses—"if he were *just* ten years younger."
You were such a darkling chime when you surfaced,

Strangelet, years later in the flow across successive moments,
at the beach, daylight bursting (just like your lungs) at the seams.
& you took the screaming air in so quiet & painfully,

the instant you burst through that roiling surf
that you were actually *here* for once, a handful of molten gold
upstretched, still somehow ticking in your palm

& you were sucked up into that forever gasp
in a full body immersion, gold pocketwatch flashing
on its 18k rope. But you were a 24k chain, weren't you?

---

65   Before I grow wings, are we really alone?· 6:04 PM, 24 Aug 2013

99.99% pure, irradiated, soft, last hot particles of sunlight.
A miracle! Aumen! Hallelujah! Just because you broke the surface
doesn't mean nobody rescued *you* from the bottom

(& you & you) such a hot, molten mess! & still,
it strikes away at your tiny 12 yr. old clapper, a single peal.
You might have unwound forever in your spools

if you hadn't closed your eyes & whispered this spell[66]:
"The People, The Peops" neon fuzz, on/off emission buzzing,
soft white meat on the inside, trembling oblivion, bells.

That same small second hand kept ticking us down
from the top. Kept dissecting each little death: earth:
in a living sequence (if you could call that living),

eyes clothed, nictitated. Nothing actually came alive
of course. Nothing but us, all bathed in a softer light,
though the creeks bubbled & jumped with fish,

granaries overflowed, cradles burst with babies.
We the Uneroded, We the Unlifted Away, these non-biodegradable
translucent plastic bags full of water & light & air,

(the ones they give out for free at the I.G.A.)
were caught in the updraft, in the April twitterlight &…Bingo!
Weeeeeee————————the Unpaused.

You always wanted this moment to last forever.
The people to be lifted away into the sky (they weren't)
toward the pink fiberglass clouds scudding overhead,

spun like cotton candy (but we weren't)
in the echo-chamber gloaming, toward that cosmic crease,
just a black tear in the sky: Hey you,

---

66   Value: On days like these I feel like a ghost haunting my own life: I have of
        late (#&wherefore_I_know_not) lost all my— · 6:06 PM, 27 Oct 2013

sing out, sing out again...
                              Wait for me, for me.
You're an emission that can't, can't be seen.
You're an immense act of combustion that goes on
goes on echoing forever, ever,

all in the same success & sequence, in the same invisible sky, (I)
echoing to the ground, even this spider, & skein, (sky)
& this moonlight between the trees

& even this moment & I myself, (& me, & me)
one cosmic brainzap torching the sticky new leaves as they unfold.
But not yet, Your Worship, not yet.

Give it a second, a century, a now: invisible skies
lifted away in plastics. There will be time to cry out the wind
when it hits an oak, unlock the yew, the you, (& you.)

Time to explode, at imago stage. Time to die.
Time to blink, little domesday clock, wade into the ocean
in sunset droves, each second a knell, a torn page, wait for it:

before you unzip the people's head, are you listening?

For the final stroke?[67] For this particularly exquisite
mongrel species of dusk? Has the wind parted us yet
into deeply blazing sapphire, into dead & living?

Has it reached past the color of liquid burning peach
into this distilled future, far into the past, far into this now,
far past the Western Union sign?

Do you see the invisible hand? Where did all the kids go?
With their glassy red eyes, where are all the pictures stored?
Will it lift *me* away too, little stranger,

---

67   Language is used to create the world · 7:24 PM, 21 Oct 2014

from this way of seeing? My wavelet, my off-key
little strike-note? To the Land of Spilled Bodies?
Why are all the mirrors drained?

Why does the looking glass hold your breath?
Why have the malls released a white cathedral glow?
The street? It's like the city was hit by a neutron bomb.

Nobody standing at the cashpoint.
So where have the bodies been delivered? In megastorms?
In tidal waves of sand? A couple extra feet on the stormbreak?

Ravaging swarms? Missing children? A rabble? Arms?
Did it all begin & end here at once, in the inflamed?
That the first day should make the last, all in an unfolded blink,

is *this* why you people are laughing as you're lifted up?

Because we all just dissolve at a touch like sunlight-rotted silk?
Because we carry our migrating deserts along behind us,
even to the ocean's edge of doom,

this prostate sky, this liquid desert,
a massive unfolding & folding, this great lifelessness.
Is that why such a sour puss? Such laughter? Such despair?[68]

Why such a complete & utter lack of light?
Even as the waves were about to break & curl down at the knees,
right at the People's Nikes, they froze

&—altogether now, in harmony, even to the edge of—
bring it: the Word, with the force of a nuke, of a domesday,
great with child, splitting its tiny silk sack...

this tolling was alone, alone, even as a boy,
always sitting at his desk in haunted music: "Thomas,
quit holdin' yourself": onely this stroke shall bear your name,

---

68   You can look right through the people but you can't tell what they're thinking
because the people evade their very own lives · 9:01 PM, Sep 23rd via web
from Weymouth, MA

unrecorded from the first syllable. This chime
paid her tax in quarters of wasted light.[69] This chime,
given back his time at manumission, shall forgive you

your innocence Mr. President,
when the final light breaks, oh yes, & all the clocks are stopped
& especially this, 150 yrs. later, she, who moved like the sea

in an argyle sweater no less, soft black hair,
black electric liquid eyes, brown-complected, freckles, a charge,
whose lips shall drink gasoline if indeed

the people are the extinction of true ice.
Full lips parted; breasts, large, of course &—& bathe away
these invisible dead stars.

Look through this tiny porthole, her black eyes,
as you lay there side by side.
Look through the locket hanging around her neck.

Right through your own sleep, into our time:
that's you, all by your lonesome. Look into this room.
Have you come to your reward?

Love of your life, walking out the door.
Maybe she's paused somewhere back there at the clinic, say,
paused for good by the people holding crosses & signs.

Maybe she's still wearing that ski-mask as she walks in,
before the procedure, drops of holy water still burning her cheek.
There you sat until after it was all over,

15 minutes late as usual, circling the block in your car.
& there you sit, after midnight once, on the parked schoolbus
for what felt like forever, staring into her,

not uttering so much as a syllable, or a chime,
soft electric joys in each warm part,
before you worked up the nerve. Didn't you kiss her?

---

69   My name is Ilse Karlner. The US turned me away at the border in 1939. I was mur-
        dered at Auschwitz · pic.twitter.com/qkD7dP4pbt · 8:25 AM, 27 Jan 2017

But *afterwards?* Didn't you say something like,
"Sneaking out of that house is like sneaking out of heaven"?
& here you sit, right now, long ago, years away, at a writing desk.

This is why the people shall always be alone,
why the people seldom consider what's feeding them
or what the people feed, like prey, like a prayer.

Seldom do the people think of the mountaintop[70]
The people have been to the mountaintop, oh yes,
to the mountaintop lifted away like a hat.

---

70   These miracles possess a physical logic: the sun bubbling away like an
      alka-seltzer in hell because once you remove the mt.top you can't put it back
      · Tue Sep 21 2010 4:31:53 PM (CDT) via web from Framingham, MA

Moonlight In the Body Of the Lyre

Stroke the Tenth: "There's another victim of the moon.
Yes, another one like me."

— MIKHAIL BULGAKOV, *Master & Margarita*

E

All of this happens behind the Gods' emptied pupil[71]
Look back over your shoulder: The Polar Ice Caps are melting for good
but tonight
        I'll disappear   into shelf after continental shelf of glacial ice
collapsing: into 2   bodies: yours   & mine.

E

So those small purple flowers on the mountainside at Delphi
                        appear in December now: a boy crawls back
into the long marble duct, decades before
                        toward the ruins of the Temple of Apollo
(though it's generally thought to be a woman   who disappears)
toward the ruins of now: 2 people are trapped   inside this moment:
                        arms & legs   entwined then disentangled,
Dis-placed by a single moon reaching us   you & I
            way down here   at sea-bed   where I'm alone:

E

One sleeps in a Las Vegas   suburb   many moons away,
as far from here as to that place where the glacial   ice is melting
once & for all,
she sleeps by herself in a single   infusion of cash to create
            liquidity, she turns
            inside his sleep
inside the desert, where she's dreaming   of a softly falling steady rain.
The West Antarctic Ice Sheet hangs like the shining blade of a guillotine
            above our neck,

---

71   As the sepulchre stone goes groaning its sky away in a cyanosis sphere: weather-
          voice in a tint of discipline & punish, fear: Roll Jordon Roll · 5:53 PM, 16 Dec 2013

his head sinking like a small river stone   in her sleep, atmospheres
down, down to the bottom of her pupil

where only the moonlight can reach, washed by cold ripples, noiseless,
                            still, but tonight
her lips are still moving, making the shape of tiny moons soundless & rising.

Now they send those bubbles up————————————————————
N_2 in the bloodstream, CO_2 particles skyward, invisible
Now they burst   one by   one   by   one————

                    E
The water cannot perjure itself like we do, They sing.
The water one man uses to make another man sing, somewhere
                      under the very same moon.
That's the single note the stream keeps repeating down below.

                    E
                    & we makes the Gods tremble
                    into a new ocean
(another victim of us)   Once that vast   white sightless eye has been
melted dark O Gods,

                    ye Gods of mine,
it can't be filled   up   again, not with glacial ice anyway,
once the black waters   swell a sudden fury far up north, & begin
to absorb the sunlight.
Daniel   Pearl's head   was   not the   head of Orpheus of course,
                    hacked from his body by the Maenads down a rush
of melted sea-ice to   warmer climes   but if you look   closely enough
tonight
at the Youtube   clip,   you can see   his lips
                  still moving...[72]

                    E
If there's a river outside your window tonight, any moving water at all,
                    wherever you may be

---

72   Maybe it was my face I saw there, reflected, drowned, unrecovered—it's 50 fadom
           deep, at sea-bed, Wi'their gold kems in their hair · 17:56 PM, 16 Dec 2013

even in a raw cement gash, a storm drain   below the bed where we used
to sleep, get up.
     Go down to it   especially under this harvest moon.
Run your fingers through the water's   broken strings,   the liquid
haruspex index.[73]
Look how instantly in a knit of ripples   then smoothed   away it heals,
smooth as a kidney's surface,   dark puce, a shining knot
                                               in the intestines, once the
                                               God's son has been hanged
trebling on the cross like a stretched-out   string melting the ice-caps,
                                               & the oceans & air currents
above them continue their 2000 year long thermohaline circulation
                                               interrupted in its guts,
the Great Ocean Conveyor Belt——for instance, in the case of undying fire,
hidden away in riddles, trapped in sky,   liquid shapes, flocks in flight,
                     for I am not gifted in the reading of birds—
     the "we" melts a desert hidden away
inside that faraway glacial ice encasing your sleep,
                     a map of the atmosphere disappears
back across the millennia
                     as it spins,   & arctic glaciers
calve & retreat forever in real-time—if—for instance, Greenland
were to melt for good, say,
                     ——————————————if a massive flood of glacial seawater,
were injected into the conveyor belt in a sudden massive shock
                              (& the gulfstreams like taut strings of gut
shifting by degree & kind)————Then by the time you took my head
into your palms, (touch this string of me
               from across the years)————
One night about a month before we————cracked, for the first & last time,
in a softer incantation of the Bacchic rites, (already the guts of a global winter
were stirring in you like a desert of dry snow), moonlight flooding
an upright mirror
                     & rippling in the fumes of unleaded gasoline,
that very moonlight already disappearing
                     with the cryosphere once it arrives.
                     Or a soundhole full of eustatic vibrations:

73   The problem with mankind at this point in history is that nothing is capable of eating us.
     Instead we eat each other. · 4:05 PM, 22 Jan 2017

That's us: a sinkhole: a planetary sink: just before the inflection point[74]
We pulled each other   blessedly apart   in black moonlight
          steaming up   from the entrails
                    of this music   it hurts—

                    E
(There was a mandolin hung above your bed with no strings)
     The infant Hermes   took a sharp   knife—
                    & cut out the turtle's insides
(Whisper it scar matter——the prophet's severed head melting by degrees)
                    This visitation was the birth of music
(in raw tonnages of life infusing   the seas, nitrogen & acids)
                    Turned our entangled bodies in bed
like the carbon molecule tattooed on your shoulder, tiny nitrogen bubbles
                    rushing upward with us
from the bottom, N:——the chemical element of atomic number 7: We^2
(Freshwater fluxes in our bloodstream——We were the fleshwater rising)
                    The infant god drilled holes in the shell
(The cataract shall flood up concurrently & then——
in a severely flesh-bound vowel, E——Go on draining us of this room)
(Eat us away from underneath——in warm currents——
                    like the massive ice-sheet on the continent)
Then taking some strings & other things lying around the cave
          He set to work measuring & fitting things together
(Whisper "if" with me: play it back——on videotape: slowly
          the tidal waves climb   & fold down at the knees: in drought,
waves of the displaced)—— If, in the end,   the flames
will not be able to resist you (& I could not) nor the floodwaters, then
Play it now in catastrophes—Play us on the Wii——& finally
finding a pair of goat's horns——(the seas shall rise from their beds)
     He attached them, pulled the seven strings neatly
                    over this beautiful invention:
                    Cranium full of greymatter gauze
                    —electricity fluid:
     black moonlight in the neural dome,
          trapped in the corpse of your eyes, tangled in your golden tresses
                    He plucked it

---

74   Which is right now. Can I block myself from accidentally living? · 12:19 AM,
       23 Aug 2014

(in refugees: in torsos like lyres: children bathing in the runoff—
gasoline fumes rising from the Omphalos Stone———you breathed into me
                              in sea-whispers
until they fall inside of the Now & the dead shall rise from their beds
                              in combers,
crash back down your cheeks,   from a thousand miles away.
                    He plucked it, She-wave, sea-currents
                    of melting:
strings at the other end of this———He plucked us a sweet new string
                    upon a peg,
this moonlight tunnel———
                    He plucked us, another victim of our bodies,
tidal pull: seawater released, breaking on the storm surge,
                    flood gates opened,
absorbing more than its share of our appetites, O Gods, ye Gods, O forests
consumed in an acid grammar   shall melt us———
                    shall melt———
the sapphire curve of this embolism-planet hanging in Pure Sleep
        in the Big Empty, this immense   waterdrop floating in space,
                    massive aquamarine globe,
                    this splash...) He plucked us.
So the taught gut vibrating   hummed & sang
        like a Swallow's note
                    & sweet music came out[75]

                    E
Only when Orpheus played his lyre
Did the burning wheel stop for a minute—

                    E
That's why the moonlight makes me feel you again so brightly.
Like wii had burned up all the O_2 in the air—& the haunted glowing pain
the only thing left to make us unrecognizable again,
                    full fathom down, alive. Why,
trapped inside this sheeted mirror, inside this skull, valuable,
scarce as platinum shining purer than pure grade uranium Yellow cake,
we conduct an even slower half-life
                    breaking down into this touch, that;

---

75   He who sings prays twice · 3:56 PM, 1 Jun 2014

this depth, unfathomed, that one unfathered,
You turn me, deep in the sleeper cell of myself, (& my torso does shine
behind this moonlight scrim the "we" decays
                                    into a newly flayed target—
into toxic assets, a shell, hydroaromatic petrolatum,
I reached out to you in eroded coastlines.
                                    The platinum sheeted pear trees
were ghostly in the orchards below. & a small river
flashed its lower voltages in broken metal strings, in cat-gut,
where they nevertheless trembled & jangled our denuded,
denatured headless trunks to be plucked down here at the ocean floor
                                    like stringless instruments—

                              E
      The Lyre of Orpheus   was a silent thing[76]
How it played the melting of the planet's immaculate white birth caul
                        softer now, soft...
How it plays the West Antarctic Ice Sheet collapsing in Legos,
                  Vaseline, Goo-Be-Gone,
                  Thomas the Tank Engine, a white bride cake:
                  plays the planet's
                  crowning. Shrinks
in warming streams inside the oceanic pull & He sings us caving it out
underwater & upward, eaten away from   the inside
                        into this planetary
whiteout   & turned you quietly out of sleep, lips
still moving in song   as you   dreamed yourself awake

                              E
Inside that brain virus, though, there was no white noise whatsoever.
      Just its own little Antarctica, its own global brain chemistry:
a massive, ruptured glacier releasing its ice-symphony into flowing
                        from below
from ice nipples, sickling chimes, inches——the slow retreat, collapse
of this planetary Sadness Center   of the Brain, Area 25——

---

76   Out the window, I saw how the planets gathered. & beyond the glassy spheres, cold
        fast streams were harnessed in the oblivion to turn the millwheels · 17:57 PM, 16
        Dec 2013

where you activated it with a finger.   Just   light it up
                                          on overdrive,
powered by the superstorm——E——
        for extinction, E for erosion,   (torso torn apart) E as in degrees
Of heat & the dull short vowel of dead   & deluge, (head torn off)
        Trouble is, you can't see it   happening in real-time——

I lie here dis placed in moonlight way   down deep, dis
membered, naturally), shimmering at Dis bed under great pressure
the ice in price calving of course, halving by 50 atmospheres at least,
the awe in cost, a smoothe sea-stone from Delphi
fit neatly inside my navel, snug.   & whispered back

the world's youngest biome vanishing in new fadoms, Dis, Dis, Dis…
new nautical leagues, sulongs: the word
You in fluid whispered, dispered
What the name Delphi actually means into my ear across all these currents—
Dolphin, (in slaughters)(or womb-rip   units)(appetites)(or yous)(or
                                          black ewes)
Put to the blade, as lesser delegates   to the oracle,

unable to afford the full temple sacrifice in specie (in species)[77]
the coin of those desolate leagues was a dispering, in disappearances no less
                    a shining cash, rare as shining glacial ice   *Ossshhhhhhhh*
Those lesser delegates once had to whisper their petitions
                              down that very same stone duct
I crawled inside of once,
decades ago, seventeen, at Delphi, just off the cruise ship.
& having vomited earlier on the worn marble steps of the Parthenon (*that*
boy, filling the skies), I crawled inside of you   all the way back

into the ruins of Apollo's temple, the ruins of   Now
all the way back into the you, I slid inside you opening

---

77   No human alive has lived through a hotter month of June: http://s;ate.me/2agBY:o ·
     12:24 PM, 20 Jul 2016

& whispered my petition in new seawater rising   rising, rising, always
on the rise,

                                down your inner ear—

                                        E
Said I went down to the sea, the sea was a-risin' Provide the music
Of what the moonlight divines tonight in oceanic wind:

Said I went down to the sea, the waters was risin'
                                (the deluge whispers back
        in the key of extinction)
                                all alone that day—
Disgorge the trees in liquid light poured severally into our ears but alone
                                I went down to the sea, the sea was a-boilin':
alone, alone,   E   demurs

in tiny sucking currents swirling at your lips————I am always alone
Said I went down to the sea, the storm cage was ragin', all alone that day—

                                        E
—a new gravity & flood of mammalian blood   drains us at sea-bed in
cold ripples
Of what our moonlight   bodies   devour:

Petrochemicals, hydrocarbons, plastics: dead oceans
                                lifted from their beds in flaring white fires
                                like the nations of the dead.
Shall pour us back down this avatar starved from within.
        Not 2 bodies (us, separated, miles   away, entwined) but a single,
malnourished,
        flensed body cannibilizing *itself* elsewhere through the torrential rains
&, in emissions,
        fluids, words, in brain-bursting chemical nebulae,
                                I crawled inside you[78]

---

78   Monarchs are one of the few insects capable of transatlantic crossing. One billion
        have disappeared since the 90's - http://www.salon.com/2015/02/10/almost_1_bil-
        lion_monarch_buttterflies_have_disappeared_since_the_1990s/...via @Salon ·
        12:53 PM, 27 Aug 2015

                 & if the moonlight makes of every tree limb a
trembling string
                Lyre   (I mean this literally),
I touched your hip out of sleep (*Touch this string or me*) exactly one moon ago
    & somewhere in Greenland   an arctic lake began to drain
through cracks in the glacial ice of its bed so that
                90 minutes later, as we slept,
3 times as much water as flows though Niagra Falls
                had flooded away into the sea,
into the butterfly-wing blue at the fringes of your iris,
into storm folds of that cataract sky,   the Dark Skies Initiative,
              those hairline fractures in glacial ice collapsing
once you opened them   up again.

               E
Slow the music of what's happening now: the burning wheel
fueled on inflows of warmer water was vibrating strings of air:

enshrouded in invisible metric tons from above, thinning ice-tongues
sheathed in hunger, in multitudes of torsos, in swallowing.

∴ in 2005, a peninsula of glacial ice the size of CA briefly melts & refreezes:

∴ in 2008, the Wilkins Ice Shelf nearly collapses, held back for now

by a shining string of ice 4 km long & trembling: Play it.

               E
Play the bivalves dissolving in seawater grown even more acidic.
Play it: one man torturing another at the black site: blacked-out eyes.
Play the air around Alcoa's smelters in TX, so acidic

it eats the galvanized coating   off barbed-wire fencing,   (Go on
eating away at the planet[79]   Bless us this day let us   consume
Give us this day   our   blessed)   & a species

---

79   & the concentric mill wheels began to turn: one minute it's night. The next, the sky
          is so wounded & open & raw, you could swallow oilpaint · 17:59 PM, 16 Dec 2013

goes extinct before it's even been discovered & named (our daily …)
    & the sea levels of course, quietly, massively (play it), rise…

E

I'm turned on the wheel inside the god's eye of your sleep
(ignition, takeoff, turn on the air)————turns its landfills, oceans,
                tankers of waste,
up one coast, down the other, non-biodegradable   plastics folded
                under layers of soil
as my lungs continue to fill the precise inverse branching of a tree
              So let us melt, Lyre, by degrees,
                at either end of this stone passage, Las Vegas,
Charlottesville, Delphi, the shining Poles——this taut moonlight string
has connected our trembling,
                a virgin seated at each end
                breathing diesel fumes.
No tear-floods nor sigh tempests move   this massive footprint
                in continents of collapsing ice,
                tonnages of carbon[80],
rising cancer rates, raw sewage, oil in the jellyfish,
                baby octopi,
                mother pelican
    washed   up in a   moonlight tide
& spreading her petroleum   slick wings—

E

Inflate my lungs. Spark the combustion. Roll, Jordan, roll.
Deflate the shape of trees into twin lyres pressed together at chest.
              Touch the strings
Shed his great dark pools at the beating cardiac   murmur,
                his nipples hardened into polar blocks,
        then melting, his body lowing separately
                on the slaughterhouse floor
                as the virgin whispers her riddle.
                You turned in my solitary cell
& breathing like a soft steady rain
                inside the desert, Lyre,
                inside your dry sleep, your wet valve,

---

80   Half of the World's Wealth Is In the Hands of Just Eight Men Study Says · TIME
          10:44 AM, 16 Jan 2017

Harmonic & simple, a sleeper, touched by cold fingers.

                          Make of this lowing in my own throat

subtracted from the polytonic scale, a moment

                              trapped in history[81] like us,

                              going taut together one last time

    then jerked up on top of me like a parachute

                              sitting up in a gravity articulated by 8 strings

into the agitated air jerked from above into this wild

                              cool cry the water still makes

         of the   moonlight below

                      E

                The global winter has come.

Sea levels   raised   like money. New coasts   carved out like capital.

Look how smooth its surface: muscle,   ice   rendered into fat

                & spilling

                a true Northwest passage at last.

I pulled out of you   (minus the touching & now, all by myself,

                in this plaster cell,

the luminous fuel of species spills out onto my stomach again,

                Lyre,

your cold missing fingers move the ocean-strings.

Not strung with gut as I am but with moonlight tonight,

                the golden tresses of the Dead.   Back down

the long stone corridor *yeah* you whispered into my ear

Come on in to the marble navel of the world

                into which that seawater shall pour

        in a soft low branching wavelength, a soft rain

spreading into the understory,   root systems,   emissions.

Simply by turning out of sleep, you refract & travel back through me,

a garment for these cold   fadoms to wear

until I've crawled into the warm clammy duct

              of your penetralia once again.

---

81   The dinosaurs had their asteroids. We have our smartphones, on which (hit enter
while walking down street) a turquoise globe emoticon spins · 4:32 PM, 10 Jun
2014 via web from Weymouth, MA

E

The oracle is at full temple price[82]
Even the seastones shall melt in this godless flood, in every cry,
in blue baby eyes, sputter-coated in moonlight,
multitudes upon multitudes in waves from displaced cities,
as God is come   to tongue & marrow,
the childrenless children are bathing in diesel therein
by scattered cattle watering in moonlight
on the boiled surfaces below,
red tags on their ears marking them for slaughter, right on schedule.
Pull back this bullock's neck.   Arch your back.   Draw the blade.
Out pours the moonlight in great pools
of light sweet crude & dark bright blood
Smoking in silver light: spills this luminous fuel
on the small of my stomach
as the sybil whispers back across the millennia *yeah*
in disappearing schools of fish   flooded coastlines   wetland washed away
financial sector underwater?
Along exhausted capillaries,
in waves of displaced refugees,   watershed tributaries
hydrocarbon-poisoned trout: through it all
a silver pool released   onto my belly spilled out
shining   milky white in the moonlight

E

Even that small river keeps repeating it down below:
E: the five fingers of the hand.
One must grow a body first   to trespass she   whispers: E, Ei, I...
Overturns its shells & stringing   & you breath out just once in your sleep,
somewhere out there,
& splash those ghost children
bound by piano wire,   strings of gut.   Unbind the bathers.
The ones swimming naked in moonlight——————one minute
They belong to you & me. The next,
(look back over your shoulder now)

---

82   The voice of one saying, Cry. And one said, What shall I cry? That death was always
necessary? · 3 min ago, 16 Dec 2013

They've been disappeared.   I'm collapsing through these sackcloth
                                ice-sheets.
Disappearing within like pure   liquid animal pain
                     Come shining under this harbinger moon
                     in strings of rising sea-levels & flesh,
the ruptured glacial ice shall give, Lyre,
when it calves, way down here,   far below   that place
                     where the flight of the eagles
Come shining & dark   will cross
                     just   one more time[83]

---

83   That's why I sign my name in fire · 3:57 AM, Sun 20 Apr 2014

Seven Tweets From the Rapture
Stroke the Eleventh

After they'd stretched my neck, a swan floated in questionmark shape, dragging the machinery of its double through brackish polluted clouds · 1:18 AM Sep 18th via web · Embed this Tweet

After the dirty bomb went off in the city & the stars disappeared like pages of math · Mon Sep 20 2010 11:03:04 (CDT) via web · Embed this Tweet

The records on the people's god were not good, which is why their dreams filled with ropes of dark smoke · Wed Sep 22 2010 10:42:26 (CDT) via web · Embed this Tweet

& I dove down deep to rescue the drowned book where it rested at the ocean floor. You were a torn out page in which the world had already been remade · 12:16 AM, 21 Nov 2013 · Embed this Tweet

You want proof? All the honeybees began to vanish at once[84] Across the radio, I hear a hive of micro-drones instead · Sat Sep 18 2010 16:42:09 (CDT) via web from Framingham, MA · Embed this Tweet

What with these death commercials & assessments of future value, no wonder we descend with the citylights slowly dissolving in stomach acid · Mon Sep 20 2010 18:01:50 (CDT) via web from Framingham, MA · Embed this Tweet

May I help you? May I help you in hell? · 11:07 PM, Sep 21st via web from Framingham, MA · Embed this Tweet

---

84   That lavender bush in bloom for example: 15 yrs ago it would have been a hive of noise. Now it fills you with a quiet fear that's deafening · 3:43 PM, Sep 18th via web from Framingham, MA

Toxic Assets
Stroke the Twelfth[85]

Vast forests have already been sacrificed
In the marble halls of the bad bank for this:
Now that portions of the glacial ice have calved to reveal stone
That hasn't been exposed for thousands of years,
In the secret history of my left eye (which turns,
incidentally, emptied & black, like the xeroxed surface of a brook),
Coastal cities simply vanish into the sea.
The planet's been knocked off its orbit by half a kilometer,
In here, behind this terraqueous globe, under great pressure,
I have stored away the tiny pearl of your face.
If I were the death of ice, I'd calve.
If I were deep waters, the birth of flesh
Would be whispered in overtones of fire.
If I were Corpus Christi, I'd simply vanish into the sea.

---

85   A little something then, for the end of the end of the world. & with that, I am
         OUTIES · 5 Dec 2013, 23:28 via web from Framingham, MA

NOTES

Regarding the quotations which appear as each section headings, I quote Browne's Miscellany Tract On Oracles: "In the Pronaos of the temple at Delphi the visitor was confronted by certain inscriptions: 'Know thyself' – 'Nothing too much' – 'Go bail and woe is at hand' – all exhortations to wisdom and prudence (Plato, Charmides, 163-4). To these is to be added, on the sole authority of Plutarch's Dialogue, the letter E, pronounced EI." For a quick read, I recommend the following link to Prickard's translation of Plutarch's notes on the ancient Greek letter E (pronounced AI) at the entrance to the Temple of Apollo: http://penelope.uchicago.edu/misctracts/plutarchE.html

"Frankenstein; or, the Presence Chamber" was written by erasing text from the novel by Mary Wollstonecraft Shelley and stitching the remaining pieces back together into a lyric about the not so slow death of glacial ice.

"The Aphasia Ward"—was written in a collaborative effort with the photographer Melania Flood, reproduced along with her photographs in Abe's Penny, and mailed to subscribers as postcards.

"Occupation: Dreamland" takes its title from the documentary film of that name directed and written by Garrett Scott and Ian Olds; Garrett Scott died at the age of 38 of a heart attack while swimming in San Diego, California, two days before the film was to win the Truer Than Fiction Award from the Independent Spirit Film Awards in Los Angeles on Saturday March 4, 2006.

"Thermal Signatures (8:46:40)": "The owl of Minerva spreads its wings only with the falling of the dusk." Hegel, preface to the Philosophy of Right. Some of the language from the first page of the poem is taken from eye-witness accounts. The material in subscript on those pages was compiled from articles written by Tom Harris, Charles Aldinger, and John Hendren. The articles themselves can be found at the following websites:

- www.science.howstuffworks.com/smart-bomb.htm
- www.aeronautics.ru/archive/vif2_project/news_0027.htm
- www.globalsecurity.org/org/news/2002/020121-attack01.htm

"Thermal Signatures (19:19)": The poem cites passages taken verbatim from Divers Voyages Touching the Discoverie of America and the Ilands Adjacent unto the Same, Made First of All by Our Englishmen and Afterwards by the Frenchmen and Britons: With Two Mappes Annexed Hereunto compiled and edited by Richard Hakluyt (1582).

The book was designed by Lesley Landis Designs

Printed in the USA
CPSIA information can be obtained
at www.ICGtesting.com
JSHW082221140824
68134JS00015B/670